Be My Disciples

Summer Program

An Alternative Model for Religious Education

Director's Guide

Peter M. Esposito
President

Jo Rotunno
Publisher

Susan Stark
Author

Cincinnati, Ohio

BeMyDisciples.com

Be My Disciples

Acknowledgments

Project Editor: Mary Malloy
Art Director: Mary Wessel
Associate Publisher: Anne Battes

Send all inquiries to:
RCL Benziger
8805 Governor's Hill Drive
Suite 400
Cincinnati, Ohio 45249

Toll Free 877-275-4725
Fax 800-688-8356
Visit us at RCLBenziger.com

978-0-7829-1674-4
Be My Disciples Summer Program

1st Printing
May 2013

Table of Contents

Welcome to *Be My Disciples!*

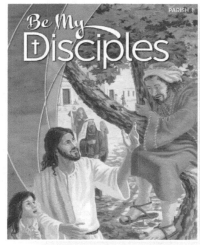
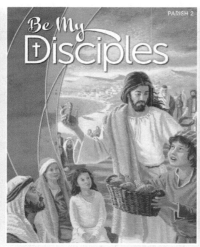
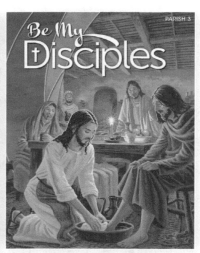
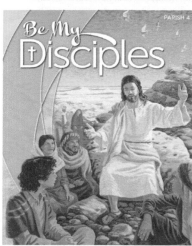
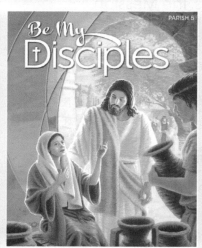
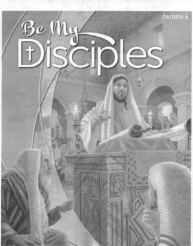

Be My Disciples

The innovative new Catholic catechetical program, adapted to facilitate as a summer program, that leads children and their families to

- grow in their conversion to Jesus Christ

- develop the habits of discipleship

- decide each day to choose life in Christ

- live as active, committed members of the Catholic Church

Be My Disciples Summer Program

The *Be My Disciples* Summer Program presents this innovative religion series in a three-week, four-hours-a-day program. Facilitating the *Be My Disciples* series during the summer months will allow you to reach a broad audience of children, parents, and families in your parish. Through the rich Roman Catholic tradition participants will be invited to become more committed disciples of Jesus Christ. *Be My Disciples* Summer Program can enrich and transform the faith life of your parish.

The most important responsibility of any parish is the sharing of faith to the next generation. For that reason, RCL Benziger always starts with the needs of the children and their families.

- What do the children need from the parish in order to grow in faith?

- What content will help the children value and grow in their Catholic faith and keep Jesus Christ at the forefront of their lives?

- What process will give them the skills they need to navigate the complexities of today's world?

- How can we reach the greatest number of children in the parish?

- How can we best help parishes partner with parents and families in the faith formation of their children?

- And, what are the creative ways we can invite the whole parish community to join with the parish's children on their faith journeys?

A Balanced Approach

Be My Disciples Summer Program shares our faith story in a catechumenal methodology that gathers both the multi-age, large group of summer participants as well as age- or grade-level groups to reflect and learn Scripture, doctrine, and prayer, and to worship together. Participants will also discover the major seasons and feasts of the Church year and explore the principles of Catholic Social Teaching. The program:

- **Invites** children to discipleship through a dynamic methodology that incorporates the latest findings in brain research, psycho-social development, and emotional intelligence;

- **Teaches**, reinforces, and extends knowledge of Scripture, Catholic doctrine, and the Church year every summer in every grade level through RCL Benziger's unique spiral structure; and

- **Challenges** children to a deeper integration of faith and life by leading them to higher levels of thinking and encouraging a daily faith-choice.

Be My Disciples Summer Program

A Child-Centered Catechesis

Be My Disciples Summer Program helps children know and live their faith through loving service to others. Each day, children gather to:

- **Grow in Knowledge.** Through RCL Benziger's unique spiral structure, children are introduced to Scripture, Catholic Tradition, and the liturgical year, and reinforce and extend their knowledge year to year.

- **Connect Faith with Their Experience.** Through a process of presentation, application, reflection, and decision, children relate knowledge of the Catholic faith to their life experiences and commit themselves more deeply to the person and mission of Jesus Christ.

- **Practice Skills of Discipleship.** By learning the gifts and qualities of discipleship and practicing its habits and virtues, children learn the skills required to follow Jesus.

- **Follow the Spiral Structure.** *Be My Disciples* Summer Program incorporates the same spiral structure into its presentation of the Catholic faith as our school-year curriculum does. As the children grow—from year to year—they revisit and expand their knowledge as new information is presented about these topics in succeeding grades. (See pages 8-9 in the *Be My Disciples* Program Director's Manual available on the Resource DVD.)

Program Features

Be My Disciples Summer Program incorporates Sacred Tradition, Sacred Scripture and the Church year in a triple spiral structure that weaves together the full story of faith during the three-week program.

Sacred Tradition

Children in grades 1–6 or in age-level groups (primary, intermediate, older children) are introduced in developmentally appropriate ways to the core concepts of Catholic Tradition through the twenty-four doctrine chapters in the student books. The six units of the *Be My Disciples* student books are organized according to the first three pillars of the *Catechism of the Catholic Church*. There are two units devoted to each of these three pillars: We Believe (our creed), We Worship (our liturgy), and We Live (our moral code).

Each of the three weeks in the Summer Program focuses on one of the first three pillars. The fourth pillar, prayer and spirituality, is incorporated throughout the program.

Sacred Scripture

Each day in the Summer Program is designed around a Scripture passage which provides an overarching theme for the day's opening and closing activities and prayer experiences.

Liturgical Year

The children have the opportunity to explore up to fifteen seasonal celebrations during the Summer Program, which incorporates these lessons into interactive learning experiences on Days 5, 10, and 15. Another option is to invite parents and other parishioners to come together for intergenerational sessions with the children that celebrate the liturgical season. The adult content for these sessions can be drawn from the reproducible pages of RCLB's *Keeping Faith First: A Resource Supporting the Whole Community of Faith.* Large and small group activities for all participants can be chosen from the lesson plans in the *Be My Disciples* catechist guides.

Provides Flexibility

Be My Disciples Summer Program is designed as a three-week, four-hour per day program. You can schedule the three weeks at a time best suited for your parish, and you can decide the daily schedule. You can combine two days into a one-day mini-retreat, or spread the sessions out over more than three weeks. A two-week program option, explained on pages 128-130 of this manual, invites parents and families to take responsibility for teaching certain chapters by using the *Be My Disciples* At Home Family Guide.

Build on, adapt, revise, and shape the session outlines provided using the gifts and creativity of your leadership team. A collaborative approach will best serve the needs of the children and families in your parish community.

Celebrates with Music

The *Be My Disciples* Summer Program takes full advantage of the *Be My Disciples* music program. A separate music CD is available for each age- or grade-level learning group. The music is incorporated into the large and small group experiences of prayer. The children will also learn the Mass parts, which they will sing during the Mass on Day 10 in the Summer Program.

Focuses on Virtues Through Disciple Power

An integral feature in *Be My Disciples* is Disciple Power, which focuses on the character formation of the learners by teaching virtues, gifts, and habits that build disciples of Jesus. Each day during the Summer Program the children will give a creative presentation of the Disciple Power virtues learned in each chapter. They will be challenged to integrate these virtues, gifts, and habits into their lives.

Be My Disciples Summer Program

Involves Parents and Families

Be My Disciples Summer Program engages the whole family and offers program leaders ideas and options for how to involve parents, families, and other members of the parish community.

Involves Adolescents and Young Adults

Junior high, high school age youth, and young adults can serve as small group helpers and discussion leaders, catechist assistants, large group activity leaders, facilitators of ice-breakers and outdoor games during break time, members of music teams, and mentors for the younger children. Many young people are looking for ways to be actively involved in their parish communities and summer is a prime-time to help make this happen.

Involves the Parish Community

Suggestions for how you can involve the broader parish community in the Summer Program sessions are provided. These suggestions include the formation of the leadership team of catechists and other volunteers, as well as facilitation of an intergenerational We Are Disciples event on the last day of the program.

The *Be My Disciples* Parish Director's Manual also contains four intergenerational gatherings, including a session in which families, with their children, can reflect on the meaning and importance of sharing faith. In addition, there are workshops for parents and families that introduce *Be My Disciples*, and explore the three Unit themes of the program.

Offers Leader Resources

A comprehensive collection of resources supports your planning and implementation of the *Be My Disciples* Summer Program.

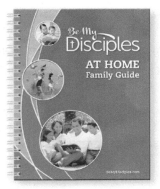

Be My Disciples At Home Family Guide

The *Be My Disciples* At Home Family Guide offers simple, easy-to-follow plans for parents and families should you choose to shorten the summer program from three weeks to two. In this scheduling format, children explore the first two chapters of each unit during the Summer Program, and parents work with their children on the last two chapters in each unit. The At Home guide provides strategies for children of various grades to proceed through their books sequentially, while also sharing family faith together.

Additional Activities

Enhance the chapter lessons with timesaving, reproducible activities that extend the children's learning.

Assessment Tools

Use reproducible masters to create an assessment portfolio with chapter and unit tests and other assessment tools.

BeMyDisciples.com

RCL Benziger offers unparalleled Web site support. Program directors, catechists, parents and families, and children all will find helpful resources. Program information, articles, enrichment activities, games, projects, and stories support growth in discipleship. Interactive chapter reviews reinforce learning, and activities and games make learning fun. With new articles and features added weekly, everyone can enjoy *BeMyDisciples*.com all year long.

In-Service Gatherings for Catechists

The *Be My Disciples* Parish Director's Manual contains two in-service session plans to use with your catechists, "From Day One" and *Echoes of Faith Plus*.

Session Features

SESSION

You can offer the Summer Program as a three-week, fifteen-day program at the parish, or as a two-week program with an At Home option.

THEME

The Scripture for each session provides a theme for reflection and sharing, and connects with the faith concepts of that day's assigned age- or grade-level chapters.

IN ADVANCE

Review this checklist of tasks that need to be completed prior to the session.

Coordinate responsibilities with your team, and provide your catechists and other leaders with resources and support.

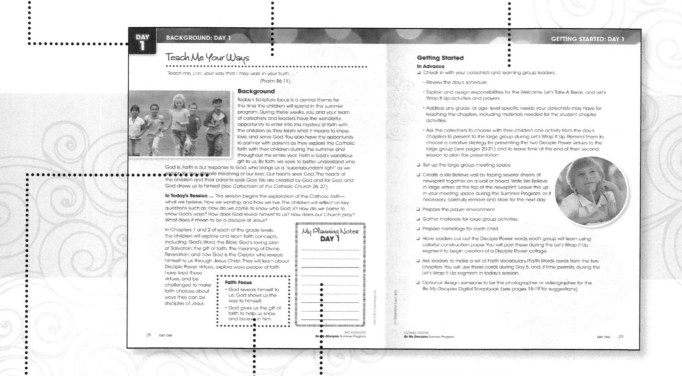

BACKGROUND

A short essay provides theological background and an overview of the chapter content that the children will be discovering in their age- or grade-level learning groups.

FAITH FOCUS

There is a clear, Scripture-based focus for the session's opening and closing prayers and activities. In addition, each of the two day's chapters has its own specific Faith Focus.

MY PLANNING NOTES

Use this space to record preparation notes about responsibilities, materials, adaptations to the session, and so forth.

MATERIALS

Catechists will need the Catechist Guide for their grade levels. Children will need their student books. Be sure to have the *Be My Disciples* Music CDs on hand for every session.

WELCOME

Provide a warm and welcoming environment from the moment the children arrive at the session. Greet parents or caretakers who come to drop off the children.

BLESS US, LORD

After the icebreaker and focusing activity, the participants pray together. Decide in advance who will lead the prayer.

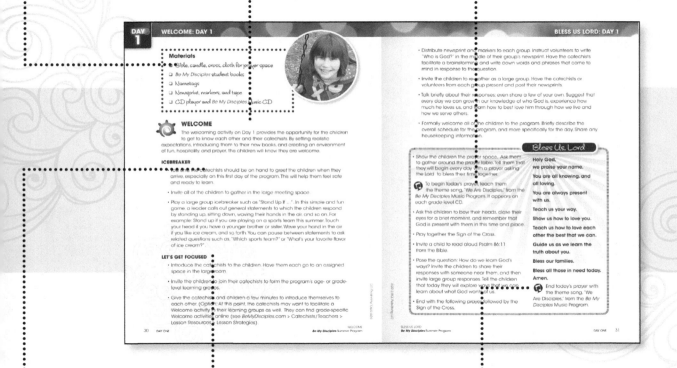

ICEBREAKER

Each session begins with a large group icebreaker. The goal is to start each session by bringing together all of the participants in a fun and interactive way.

LET'S GET FOCUSED

This activity will focus the children on the overall theme for the session, and transitions into the opening prayer. Adapt the process to best meet the needs of your group.

MUSIC

Each of the large group prayer experiences includes music from the *Be My Disciples* Music Program. In addition, encourage your leaders to use the grade-specific music CDs in their learning groups throughout the sessions.

Session Features

Allow up to 1 hour for DISCOVER, Part One activities.

DISCOVER, Part One
Introduce

Each week of the Summer Program focuses on one of three major themes. Every day, before the children meet in their age- or grade-level learning groups, you can introduce, reinforce, and build on the week's theme using the We Believe, We Worship, or We Live walls.

Allow up to 1 hour, 15 minutes for DISCOVER, Part Two activities.

DISCOVER, Part Two
Introduce

Have the participants gather as a large group after the break, and invite them to name some of their learning from the day's first chapter.

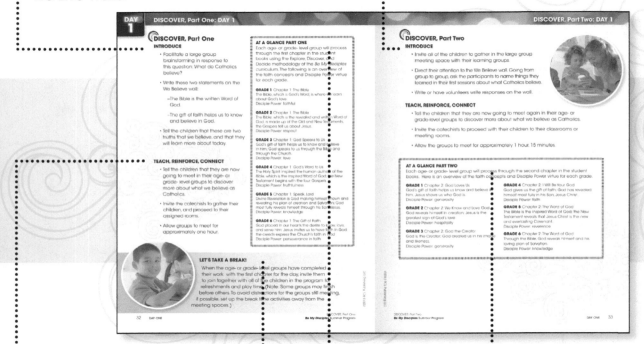

TEACH, REINFORCE, CONNECT

The children meet in their age- or grade- level groups to explore a chapter. On Days 5, 10, and 15, the children participate in Activity Centers using the Enriching the Lesson, Catholic Social Teaching, and Liturgical Year lessons, or We Celebrate Mass. (Mass is celebrated on Day 10.)

LET'S TAKE A BREAK!

Provide refreshments and opportunity for play during the break. If youth from the parish are volunteering with the Summer Program, invite them to facilitate a few organized games or ask them to help supervise free play.

AT A GLANCE: Part One and Part Two

The At A Glance chart enables the catechists and you to take a quick look at the faith concepts covered in each grade level for the day's first and second chapters.

LET'S WRAP IT UP
REINFORCE

Participants name things they learned in the day's second chapter and add to the We Believe, We Worship or We Live walls.

WE PRAY

To conclude the session, choose a prayer from one of the grade-level books or use the prayer provided, which is based on the session's Scripture theme. Over the course of the three weeks, invite the age- or grade-level learning groups to be responsible for leading the closing prayer.

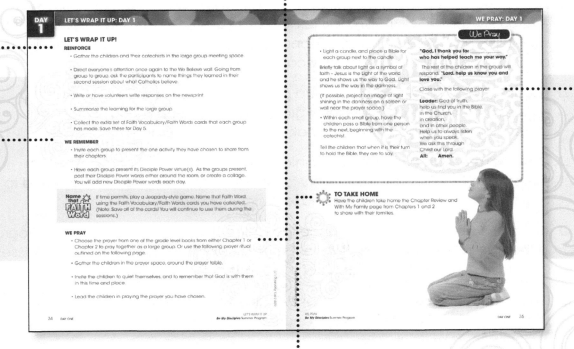

WE REMEMBER

The age- or grade-level groups present an activity from one of the day's chapters. They also present their Disciple Power virtues. If the group has chosen to complete a week-long project (see Activity Options on pages 18-19) it can provide a status report. This time might also include volunteers sharing the Faith Choices they made and games that review Faith Vocabulary/Faith Words.

TO TAKE HOME

Each day the children take home the Chapter Review and With My Family pages from the chapters taught in that day's sessions.

Leader's Toolbox

Advance Preparation
Taking the First Steps

Here are some key decisions and considerations you'll want to make as you begin planning the Summer Program.

❑ **Summer Program Director.** The *Be My Disciples* Summer Program Director can be the Director of Religious Education, another parish staff member, or a qualified volunteer familiar with the parish catechetical process.

❑ **Three-week or Two-week + At Home Model.** Decide which model you will offer—the three-week model or the two-week + At Home model.

❑ **Dates and times.** When will you hold the program? Consider mornings (8:30 AM – 12:30 PM or 9 AM – 1 PM) or afternoons (1 PM – 5 PM). Decide if you want to schedule the times for Days 5, 10, and 15 differently so that parents, families, and other members of the community can participate.

❑ **Facility.** You will need a large group gathering space and smaller learning spaces for the age- or grade-level groups. Access to an outdoor area for recreation during the session's break is also a big plus.

❑ **Collaborate with Parish Staff.** Contact the pastor, school principal, youth minister and other pastoral leaders to introduce the Summer Program and to begin coordination of support and resources.

❑ **Advertise the Program.** Announce the dates and times of the Summer Program in the parish bulletin, newsletter, on the parish Web site, and at Sunday Masses. Be sure to do so well in advance of the Summer Program's start date.

❑ **Begin Registration.** Send e-vites and mail households of prospective participants a program invitation and registration materials.

❑ **Order *Be My Disciples* materials.** Each child will need a student book. Your catechists will need Catechist Guides for their respective age- or grade-levels. If you are sponsoring the two-week program, each family will need the *Be My Disciples* At Home Family Guide. Be sure to include the cost of this guide in your participant fees for the program. Also, be sure to order the *Be My Disciples* Music Program, and the Additional Activities and Assessment Booklets.

❑ **Recruit leadership.** Recruit catechists, assistants, music leaders, and additional volunteers who can help with Activity Centers (Days 5, 10, 15), snacks and games, and childcare for the younger children of volunteers. (See page 15 for more information.)

©2013 RCL Publishing LLC

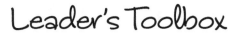

❑ **Form the Learning Groups.** Once the children have registered, determine if you have enough children for six grade-level learning groups. If not, consider combining grade levels to form age-level groups. If you choose this approach, you could rotate texts year-to-year within a particular age group. The first summer, for example, you would use the Grade 1 text, and the following summer the Grade 2 text.

❑ **Send a Program Schedule to Participating Families.** Include basic information about the program, such as days and times, and any special information about Days 5, 10, and 15.

Forming the Leadership Team

Here are suggestions for the leadership roles you will want to consider as you plan the Summer Program. (See the Parish Director's Manual, pages 16-17, for suggestions on how to recruit catechists.)

❑ **Catechists and Co-Leaders**

The catechists' primary responsibility is to prepare for and teach the chapter lessons from the *Be My Disciples* program. They also participate in large group activities and in planning the Activity Centers for Days 5, 10, and 15. Recruit co-leaders to work alongside the catechists and assist in planning, preparing, and facilitating the learning groups. The number of participants will help you determine the number of catechists and co-leaders you will need.

❑ **Activity Leaders**

Consider recruiting parish youth to assist your catechists, and to help facilitate the large group and Let's Take A Break activities.

❑ **Music Leaders**

Music leaders will add much to the Summer Program experience. Fun, engaging music draws in the children and serves as a tool for gathering them together as a large group. Music is also integral to each day's prayer experiences, and to the celebration of the Mass on Day 10.

❑ **Snack Assistants**

These helpers organize and prepare snacks for the children. They can also assist with the potluck meals (optional) on Days 5, 10 and 15.

Team Orientation and Planning

Orientation for your leadership team can include an introduction to catechetical ministry and skills for catechists, as well as an introduction to the *Be My Disciples* curriculum. You will also want to highlight the unique elements that are a part of the Summer Program.

Leader's Toolbox

Orientation to *Be My Disciples*

- ❑ **Leadership Team Workshop** Offer in-service sessions for your catechists and leaders. The *Be My Disciples* Parish Director's Manual contains two in-service session plans that you can use with your catechists and leaders. The From Day One Catechist workshop (PDM, page 63) is a three-hour DVD-assisted orientation to the catechetical ministry and to *Be My Disciples*. The workshop is divided into three parts which you can offer as three separate workshops or as a single three-hour event.

- ❑ **Summer Program Overview** Highlight the unique elements of the *Be My Disciples* Summer Program using the Overview (see pages 5-9). Review the basic process of each day and the Activity Centers the team will organize for Days 5, 10, and 15.

- ❑ **Session Overview** Walk through the parts of a session using the Session Features (see pages 10-13). Identify the parts of each session that involve special planning. Invite creative suggestions from your team.

- ❑ **Lesson Planner Ideas** Use Lesson Plan Ideas on pages 22-23 to illustrate options for how catechists can process the two chapters that are a part of a day's session. Encourage the catechists to facilitate at least one small group prayer experience with their children each day.

Team Preparation and Planning

- ❑ **Review the sessions.** Review each session's four-hour plan, and assign specific responsibilities (for prayer, activities, etc.).

- ❑ **Plan for Days 5, 10, and 15.** Review the Enriching the Learning activities that appear in the Catechist Guides, as well as the Catholic Social Teaching activities and Liturgical Year lessons. Use these activities to map out a plan for the Activity Centers for Days 5, 10, and 15. Emphasize creativity when planning these days.

- ❑ **Provide Additional Resources.** Direct leaders to the *Be My Disciples* resources available for their use. These include the Music Program, Additional Activities and Assessment booklets, the At Home Family Guide, and *BeMyDisciples*.com.

- ❑ **Establish Rules of Behavior.** Children need to know what is expected of them. Rules based on cooperation and respect give children a sense of security and belonging. Establish simple rules such as "Respect each other" and "Take care of parish property." The leadership team should model behaviors that reflect the rules.

Responsibilities

Who is responsible for what? Consider assigning the following responsibilities to team members.

TASK	PERSON(S) RESPONSIBLE
❏ Facility setup	_____
❏ Icebreakers	_____
❏ Large group activities	_____
❏ Opening Prayer	_____
❏ Closing Prayer	_____
❏ Snacks	_____
❏ Break Time	_____
❏ Music	_____
❏ Taking pictures	_____
❏ Gathering materials	_____
❏ _____	_____
❏ _____	_____
❏ _____	_____

Leader's Toolbox

Planning a Session...Considerations

Materials
Review the session plan far enough in advance so that you have plenty of time to gather materials for it. Keep in mind any session adaptations you and your team may make, and any additional materials these changes call for.

Welcome!
Draw the children into the large meeting space with music and images. Make the room look warm and inviting. Greet the participants.

Use the suggested icebreaker or substitute another activity.

Prayer Experiences
Two large group prayer experiences are a part of each day's session. Encourage catechists to use one of the prayer experiences from their two chapters with the children in their learning groups.

Prayer Environment
Prepare a prayer space for the large group and encourage your catechists to create prayer tables in their learning spaces. See the Parish Director's Manual, pages 24-31 and/or page 28 of the Catechist Guides for suggestions.

Prayer Leaders
Consider assigning responsibility for preparing and leading each of the large group prayers to one of the learning groups. A group could take responsibility for both the opening and closing prayer for the same day. Plan this in advance with your leadership team.

Music
Each prayer includes music from the *Be My Disciples* Music Program. A music team will enhance the children's experience, especially when the community celebrates Mass together on Day 10. Page 31 of the Program Director's Manual offers further suggestions regarding incorporating music into prayer.

Project and Activity Options
Here are a few ideas for projects that the learning groups could work on during the course of the program. Catechists could choose one project for each week, or one project that their learning groups would work on throughout the three-week program.

• *Be My Disciples* Digital Scrapbook
Create a digital scrapbook of your Summer Program by taking digital photos and videos all throughout the sessions. Have the slideshow or video playing the next day in the large group meeting space, accompanied with music from the *Be My Disciples* Music Program. This will help focus the children as they enter the session, and will serve as a visual reinforcement of the previous

©2013 RCL Publishing LLC

day's lessons and activities. Use the Digital Scrapbook as a part of the Day 15 concluding activities to both summarize and celebrate your time together.

• Video Project
Learning groups can prepare and present a news-documentary style video including highlights from each day's session, a collage of the activities they worked on, a dramatic presentation of one of the Bible stories they read, a biographic glimpse at the Faith-Filled People they learned about, or interviews of other participants and parishioners about their experiences of Church.

• Storybook
Learning groups could write a storybook based on a particular theme such as the Disciple Power virtues, the people or groups in The Church Follows Jesus, or the My Faith Choices they are making during the course of program.

• Comic Book, Comic Strip, or Graphic Novel
In this variation of the Storybook project, children could create any of the above based on a particular chapter or theme.

• Advertizing Campaign
Invite the children to develop an ad in a magazine, poster advertisement, billboard, TV or radio ad, jingle or song about the theme for the week ("We Believe", "We Worship", or "We Live") Their campaign could express what they learned during the course of a day or during the entire program.

• Creative Art
Have the learning group create a mosaic, collage, mural, slideshow, or photo essay that expresses their learning.

• Music
Invite those who are musically inclined to write, rewrite, select, and sing songs, or to put music with images that convey a particular message or theme.

DISCOVER, Part One and Part Two
During this part of the session, the participants meet in their age- or grade-level learning groups with a catechist. The Lesson Plan Ideas on pages 22-23 will help the catechists become familiar with the lesson process for the day's two chapters.

LET'S TAKE A BREAK
Provide children with outdoor games and the items needed in order to play those games. Recruit youth from the parish to facilitate the games.

LET'S WRAP IT UP
Pages 20-21 explain the Disciple Power feature and offer activity suggestions for catechists and group leaders as they plan their daily Disciple Power virtue presentation. A list of the Disciple Power virtues for each day of the Summer Program, by grade level, is also provided on pages 134-135.

Leader's Toolbox

Disciple Power

An integral feature of *Be My Disciples* is Disciple Power, which focuses on the character formation of the learners by teaching virtues, Gifts and Fruits of the Holy Spirit, and habits that help build disciples. The Disciple Power feature helps the children grow in their understanding of what it means to follow Jesus, and to integrate these virtues, gifts, and habits into their lives. These will serve them well on their lifelong journey as disciples of Jesus Christ.

Each chapter in *Be My Disciples* features one Disciple Power virtue. In the *Be My Disciples* Summer Program, the children learn about two Disciple Power virtues each day (excepting days 5, 10, and 15). During the Let's Wrap It Up segment of the day's session, the learning groups are invited to present one or both of the virtues they learned about that day to the larger group. (Note: A complete list of the Disciple Power virtues is provided on pages 134-135.) Here are some simple ideas catechists can use with the children for presenting the Disciple Power virtues in engaging and creative ways.

Disciple Power Activity Suggestions

One-Minute Skits

Have the children perform impromptu skits that demonstrate both practice of the virtue and the practice of its opposite. For example, have them show patience while waiting in line at the amusement park, and then impatience.

Charades and Pantomimes

The children can work in pairs or small groups to demonstrate a virtue without using words. The object is for the large group to guess the virtue.

Mural or Collage

Over the course of the three weeks, age- or grade-level groups can contribute to a large mural or collage which illustrates the Disciple Power virtues.

Sing-along Songs

Use the melody of simple, familiar songs to quickly write a jingle about the virtues. Your group can teach the jingle to the large group.

Twenty-questions

The large group can ask up to twenty "yes" or "no" questions in an effort to discover what the Disciple Power virtue is.

Cinquains

Have the children work together to write a cinquain that describes the Disciple Power virtue. A cinquain is a five-line poem that describes the word. Here are two variations:

Line 1: the one-word Disciple Power virtue
Line 2: two words that describe the virtue
Line 3: three words that describe actions related to the virtue
Line 4: four words that describe the feelings related to the virtue
Line 5: one word that is a synonym or another name for the virtue

Line 1: the Disciple Power virtue
Line 2: a four syllable description of the virtue
Line 3: a six syllable description of the virtue
Line 4: an eight syllable description of the virtue
Line 5: repeat the Disciple Power virtue

Acrostic Poems

An acrostic poem uses the letters in a word to describe the word. A simple acrostic uses the letters in the word to begin each line of the poem.

Quick Word or Picture Games

If you run short on time and need a quick and easy way to present your Disciple Power virtues for the day, try simple word or picture games such as:

Unscramble the Word. Simply have one of the children in your group write the word scrambled on the board or newsprint for the large group to unscramble.

Draw a Virtue. Write the Disciple Power words for the day on index cards, and call for volunteers to come to the front of the room. Have them look at the virtue on the card, and quickly draw a picture of it. The person who can draw the picture from which the large group can correctly guess the word "wins."

Leader's Toolbox

Lesson Plan Ideas

Two of the benefits of sponsoring a Summer Program are the flexibility and opportunity for enhanced creativity in catechesis it provides. Here's a look at one of the *Be My Disciples* chapter Lesson Planners with a few ideas for adaptation.

FOCUS

The focuses for the day's two chapters will most often be closely related. One option is to combine the two lessons into one. This may leave more time to work on projects, or to spend more time with an activity.

EXPLORE

The children will have participated in large group prayer to open the session. Catechists may wish to move directly into the Reflect process on the first student page rather than begin with the prayer.

DISCOVER

On The Church Follows Jesus page the participants will learn about a Saint, holy person, or ministry that illustrates discipleship. Invite guest speakers whose ministries exemplify discipleship to address the children at the beginning of the Discover portion of the day's session.

DISCIPLE POWER

Each learning group will explore two Disciple Power virtues each day. They will present their virtues to the large group in the Let's Wrap It Up session. The catechist could forego one of the chapter's activities in order to have more time to prepare the Disciple Power presentations. See activity suggestions on pages 20-21.

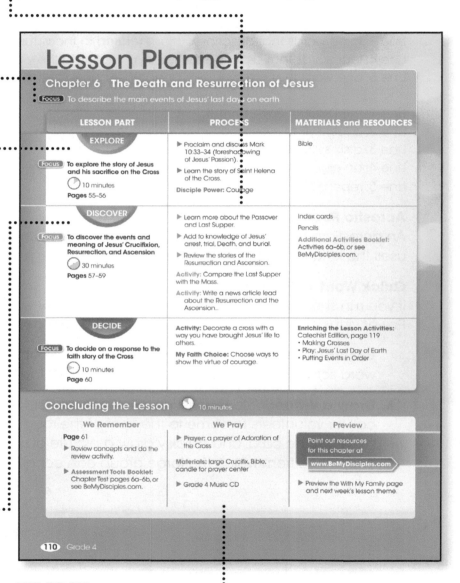

WE PRAY

Catechists should facilitate at least one of the prayer experiences each day in their learning groups. Learning groups can present one of the day's We Pray prayers in lieu of the large group closing prayer, or as an activity during Let's Wrap It Up. If a group's chapter prayer is to learn a prayer in sign language, they could teach that prayer to the large group. If the chapter prayer describes how to pray with gestures or in another language, the children can teach and pray that prayer with the large group.

ACTIVITIES

The flexibility of Summer Program allows for activity-rich sessions. Catechists can pick and choose from the activities in the day's two chapters, to spend more time on some and less on others, or expand the activities into creative projects. The learning groups will share one activity each day during the Let's Wrap It Up session. Suggest that, over the course of the three weeks, groups present a variety of types of activities (see pages 18-19 for additional suggestions).

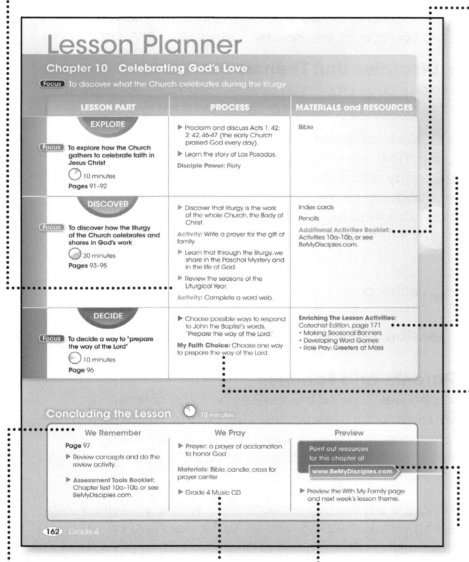

ADDITIONAL ACTIVITIES BOOKLET

These activities can be facilitated in addition to, or instead of activities in the student book. The children could also take the activities home and complete them with their families.

ENRICHING THE LESSON ACTIVITIES

Use these activities on Days 5, 10, and 15 of the three-week program as the basis for Activity Centers and the Interactive Gallery that showcases the children's work. Plan in advance which activities and how many activities you will need.

MY FAITH CHOICE

Children can complete both My Faith Choice pages during the session, or take them home to talk about with their parents.

BeMyDisciples.com

Encourage the catechists to explore *BeMyDisciples*.com. If computers are available for the children, the catechists can facilitate chapter reviews and various online activities with the children. If possible, provide a "live" orientation to *BeMyDisciples*. com when you meet with your leadership team.

WE REMEMBER

If time is limited, participants can take this page home to complete on their own or with their families.

GRADE LEVEL MUSIC CDs

Encourage the catechists to use the *Be My Disciples* Music CDs with their groups.

WITH MY FAMILY

Be sure the children go home with the With My Family pages from the day's two chapters.

Leader's Toolbox

Workshops for Parents and Families

Introduction to *Be My Disciples*

This workshop, which is included in the Parish Director's Manual, page 92, provides a two-hour, video-assisted orientation to *Be My Disciples* for adult members of the children's families. The video component of the workshop is the *Be My Disciples* awareness video. This video is included on the *Be My Disciples* Program Resource DVD. If you do not have this DVD, you can obtain one by calling 1-877-275-4725.

Introduction to *Be My Disciples* Unit Themes

Three ninety-minute sessions are provided in the Parish Director's Manual (see page 95) to help you introduce the three major unit themes of *Be My Disciples* to adults.

Ideally, you would offer these sessions just before the children begin their study of each unit. For example, during the three-week Summer Program, you could hold these workshops on the Sunday afternoons during the three weeks. The first session, We Believe, would be scheduled for the Sunday prior to the beginning of the program. It would introduce parents to the theme that their children will be exploring all during that first week. You could then hold the remaining two sessions on the following two Sundays.

The three parent sessions, which correspond to the three weeks of the Summer Program are:

Session 1: We Believe • Session 2: We Worship • Session 3: We Live

Invite and Welcome Parents and Families

Make a special effort to invite and welcome all the families bringing children to the Summer Program. As you register families, be sensitive to those in diverse situations—single parents, grandparents raising grandchildren, children being raised by caregivers, or families struggling with economic or other hardships.

As Volunteers

Invite parents to volunteer during the three-week sessions. Offer simple ways they can help out, including providing snacks, helping with set-up or clean-up, or helping with administrative tasks that could be done on their own time prior to and during the Summer Program. Parents and other adults in the parish community have gifts and talents well-suited to the leadership needs of the program.

As Participants

Encourage parents to come to the program on Days 5, 10, and 15. Invite them to participate in the Mass on Day 10, and in any other intergenerational gatherings (such as potluck meals) you schedule as a part of these sessions.

Resources for Parents

Provide Resources

Be My Disciples offers numerous resources to support and encourage parents in their role in the faith formation of their children. These include:

With My Family Pages

The With My Family page that ends each chapter assists the family in guiding faith formation at home. It includes a summary of the chapter's doctrine concepts, suggestions for reading the Bible at home, ideas for family activities and a spirituality feature. The children will take the With My Family pages home after each session.

Chapter and Unit Reviews

Because of the intensive Summer Program schedule, the children will not always complete the Chapter Reviews or Unit Reviews while at the parish. Send these pages home so that parents can guide their children in completing them.

Assessment Tools and Additional Activities

These reproducible materials enhance the lessons and extend the children's learning. Parents can work with their children at home using these tools.

Be My Disciples At Home Family Guide

This at home companion to the *Be My Disciples* program helps parents teach or reinforce the content of the children's text. If you choose the two-week + At Home model for your summer program, each family will need a copy of this guide.

BeMyDisciples.com

This Web site offers the best possible support for children and families. Content of this extensive and easy-to-use site includes creative resources such as children's activities and games, interactive chapter reviews, a weekly continuing story, a Saints resource, a tour of a Catholic Church, Gospel reflections, and other resources for children, parents and catechists.

TIP!! Include an orientation or "tour" of *BeMyDisciples*.com as a part of one of the intergenerational gatherings or parent workshops you schedule for the *Be My Disciples* program.

Be My Disciples Week One Overview

WEEK ONE: We Believe

Background

There is one God who is Father, Son, and Holy Spirit. This doctrine of the Holy Trinity is the central mystery of our faith. During Week One, you will invite the children to explore their personal faith and the faith of the Church.

Using the first two units of the *Be My Disciples* curriculum, We Believe: Part One and We Believe: Part Two, you will lead the participants through a process that engages their life experiences and grounds each day's content in Scripture. On Day 5, the children will participate in Activity Centers and an Interactive Gallery or showcase to extend and reinforce the week's learning. These activities are chosen from the Enriching the Lesson, Catholic Social Teaching, and Liturgical Year activities in the Catechist Guides.

KEY FAITH CONCEPTS

- **The Gift of Faith**
- **God the Creator**
- **Jesus the Messiah**
- **The Holy Spirit**
- **The Holy Trinity**
- **The Communion of Saints**
- **The Church**

The Church Teaches ...

The *General Directory for Catechesis* (GDC) reminds us:

> [Our] "Yes" to Jesus Christ, who is the fullness of the Revelation of the Father, is twofold: a trustful abandonment to God and a loving assent to all that he has revealed to us. This is possible only by means of the action of the Holy Spirit. *GDC* 38

Further Reading and Reflection

For more on the teachings of the Catholic Church on the mysteries of Divine Revelation and the faith we profess, see *Catechism of the Catholic Church* 26-1065 and *United States Catholic Catechism for Adults*, pages 1-162.

DAILY HIGHLIGHTS

Days 1-4   Each four-hour session includes warm-up and focusing activities, prayer celebrations, and age- or grade-level learning groups in which the children explore chapters from Unit 1 and Unit 2 in the *Be My Disciples* student book. The sessions include a break for fun and refreshments. Let's Wrap It Up concludes each session with presentations of activities, Disciple Power virtues, and closing prayer.

Week One WE BELIEVE	Day 1 Teach Me Your Ways	Day 2 Great is the Lord	Day 3 Jesus, the Messiah	Day 4 Go and Make Disciples	Day 5 I Believe!
Scripture	Psalm 86:11	Luke 1:46-47	Matthew 16:16	Matthew 28:19-20	John 20:26–31
Faith Focus	• God reveals himself to us; God shows us the way to himself. • God gives us the gift of faith to help us know and believe in him.	• God reveals himself and his loving plan of creation and Redemption. • As Jesus' disciples, we proclaim God's greatness when we say "yes" to God through our words and actions.	• Jesus is the Son of God, the Messiah. • The Paschal Mystery is the mystery of Jesus' Passion, Death, Resurrection and Ascension.	• Jesus promised that God the Father and he would send the Holy Spirit. • The Church is the People of God. • We belong to the Catholic Church, the Body of Christ. The Church lives out the command of Jesus to "Go make disciples."	• The Church professes belief in the Holy Trinity. • We celebrate the liturgical seasons of Advent, Christmas and Ordinary Time. **Liturgical Year:** Advent, Christmas, Epiphany, Ordinary Time **Catholic Social Teaching:** Care for God's creation; Call to family, community, and participation
Discover, Part One	Learning Groups • Chapter 1	Learning Groups • Chapter 3	Learning Groups • Chapter 5	Learning Groups • Chapter 7	Activity Centers •Enriching the Lesson •Catholic Social Teaching •Liturgical Year
Discover, Part Two	Learning Groups • Chapter 2	Learning Groups • Chapter 4	Learning Groups • Chapter 6	Learning Groups • Chapter 8	Activity Centers •Enriching the Lesson •Catholic Social Teaching •Liturgical Year
Let's Wrap It Up	• Activity sharing • Disciple Power presentations	• Activity sharing • Disciple Power presentations	• Activity sharing • Disciple Power presentations	• Activity sharing • Disciple Power presentations	Interactive Gallery • Displays • Presentations Closing Prayer

Day 5

Activity Centers On this day, the children will participate in Activity Centers. These activities are chosen from the Enriching the Lesson, Catholic Social Teaching, and Liturgical Year activities in the Catechist Guides for Units 1 and 2.

Interactive Gallery The Interactive Gallery is a culmination of the day's work, complete with displays and presentations by the children for the children. You may also want to include projects and activities from the previous days' sessions in this showcase. Invite parents, other family members, and parishioners to participate in the day. Adapt and design the session to best fit the needs and resources of your group.

Teach Me Your Ways

"Teach me, Lord, your way that I may walk in your truth, . . ."

(Psalm 86:11)

Background

Today's Scripture focus is a central theme for the time the children will spend in this summer program. During these weeks, you and your team of catechists and leaders have the wonderful opportunity to enter into the mystery of faith with the children as they learn what it means to know, love, and serve God. You also have the opportunity to partner with parents as they explore the Catholic faith with their children during the summer and throughout the entire year. Faith is God's wondrous gift to us. By faith, we seek to better understand who God is. Faith is our response to God, who brings us a "superabundant light" as we search for the ultimate meaning of our lives. Our hearts seek God. The hearts of the children and their parents seek God. We are created by God and for God, and God draws us to himself (see *Catechism of the Catholic Church* 26, 27).

In Today's Session ... This session begins the exploration of the Catholic faith—what we believe, how we worship, and how we live. The children will reflect on key questions such as: How do we come to know who God is? How do we come to know God's ways? How does God reveal himself to us? How does our Church pray? What does it mean to be a disciple of Jesus?

In Chapters 1 and 2 of each of the grade levels, the children will explore and learn faith concepts, including: God's Word, the Bible; God's loving plan of Salvation; the gift of faith; the meaning of Divine Revelation; and how God is the Creator who reveals himself to us through Jesus Christ. They will learn about Disciple Power virtues, explore ways people of faith have lived those virtues, and be challenged to make faith choices about ways they can be disciples of Jesus.

Faith Focus

- God reveals himself to us; God shows us the way to himself.

- God gives us the gift of faith to help us know and believe in him.

My Planning Notes DAY 1

_____

_____

_____

_____

_____

_____

_____

_____

_____

Getting Started

In Advance

❑ Check in with your catechists and learning group leaders.

   • Review the day's schedule.

   • Explain and assign responsibilities for the Welcome, Let's Take A Break, and Let's Wrap It Up activities and prayers.

   • Address any grade- or age- level specific needs your catechists may have for teaching the chapters, including materials needed for the student chapter activities.

   • Ask the catechists to choose with their children one activity from the day's chapters to present to the large group during Let's Wrap It Up. Remind them to choose a creative strategy for presenting the two Disciple Power virtues to the large group (see pages 20-21) and to leave time at the end of their second session to plan the presentation.

❑ Set up the large group meeting space.

❑ Create a We Believe wall by taping several sheets of newsprint together on a wall or board. Write We Believe in large letters at the top of the newsprint. Leave this up in your meeting space during the Summer Program, or, if necessary, carefully remove and store for the next day.

❑ Prepare the prayer environment. Consider having the learning groups share the prayer responsibility throughout the three weeks.

❑ Gather materials for large group activities.

❑ Prepare nametags for each child.

❑ Have leaders cut out the Disciple Power words each group will learn using colorful construction paper. You will post these during the Let's Wrap It Up segment to begin creation of a Disciple Power collage.

❑ Ask leaders to make a set of Faith Vocabulary/Faith Words cards from the two chapters. You will use these cards during Day 5, and, if time permits, during the Let's Wrap It Up segment in today's session.

❑ Optional: Assign someone to be the photographer or videographer for the *Be My Disciples* Digital Scrapbook (see pages 18-19 for suggestions).

Materials

- ☐ Bible, candle, cross, cloth for prayer space
- ☐ *Be My Disciples* student books
- ☐ Nametags
- ☐ Newsprint, markers, and tape
- ☐ CD player and *Be My Disciples* Music CD

WELCOME

The welcoming activity on Day 1 provides the opportunity for the children to get to know each other and their catechists. By setting realistic expectations, introducing them to their new books, and creating an environment of fun, hospitality, and prayer, the children will know they are welcome.

ICEBREAKER

- You and the catechists should be on hand to greet the children when they arrive, especially on this first day of the program. This will help them feel safe and ready to learn.

- Invite all of the children to gather in the large meeting space.

- Play a large group icebreaker such as "Stand Up If …". In this simple and fun game, a leader calls out general statements to which the children respond by standing up, sitting down, waving their hands in the air, and so on. For example: Stand up if you are playing on a sports team this summer. Touch your head if you have a younger brother or sister. Wave your hand in the air if you like ice cream, and so forth. You can pause between statements to ask related questions such as, "Which sports team?" or "What's your favorite flavor of ice cream?"

LET'S GET FOCUSED

- Introduce the catechists to the children. Have them each go to an assigned space in the large room.

- Invite the children to join their catechists to form the program's age- or grade-level learning groups.

- Give the catechists and children a few minutes to introduce themselves to each other. (Option: At this point, the catechists may want to facilitate a Welcome activity in their learning groups as well. They can find grade-specific Welcome activities online (see *BeMyDisciples*.com > Catechists/Teachers > Lesson Resources > Lesson Strategies).

- Distribute newsprint and markers to each group. Instruct volunteers to write "Who is God?" in the middle of their group's newsprint. Have the catechists facilitate a brainstorming and write down words and phrases that come to mind in response to the question.

- Invite the children to re-gather as a large group. Have the catechists or volunteers from each group present and post their newsprints.

- Talk briefly about their responses; even share a few of your own. Suggest that every day we can grow in our knowledge of who God is, experience how much he loves us, and learn how to best love him through how we live and how we serve others.

- Formally welcome all of the children to the program. Briefly describe the overall schedule for the program, and more specifically for the day. Share any housekeeping information.

Bless Us, Lord

- Show the children the prayer space. Ask them to gather around the prayer table. Tell them that they will begin every day with a prayer asking the Lord to bless their time together.

- To begin today's prayer, teach them the theme song, "We Are Disciples," from the *Be My Disciples* Music Program. It appears on each grade level CD.

- Ask the children to bow their heads, close their eyes for a brief moment, and remember that God is present with them in this time and place.

- Pray together the Sign of the Cross.

- Invite a child to read aloud Psalm 86:11 from the Bible.

- Pose the question: What are the ways we learn about God? Invite the children to share their responses with someone near them, and then invite large group responses. Tell the children that today they will explore ways that we can learn about what God wants of us.

- End with the following prayer, followed by the Sign of the Cross.

**Holy God,
we praise your name.**

You are all knowing, and all loving.

You are always present with us.

Teach us your way.

Show us how to love you.

Teach us how to love each other the best that we can.

Guide us as we learn the truth about you.

Bless our families.

Bless all those in need today. Amen.

End today's prayer with the theme song, "We Are Disciples," from the *Be My Disciples* Music Program.

DISCOVER, Part One

INTRODUCE

- Facilitate a large group brainstorming in response to this question: What do Catholics believe?

- Write these two statements on the We Believe wall:

    – The Bible is the written Word of God.

    – The gift of faith helps us to know and believe in God.

- Tell the children that these are two truths that we believe, and that they will learn more about today.

TEACH, REINFORCE, CONNECT

- Tell the children that they are now going to meet in their age- or grade- level groups to discover more about what we believe as Catholics.

- Invite the catechists to gather their children, and proceed to their assigned rooms.

- Allow groups to meet for approximately one hour.

AT A GLANCE PART ONE

Each age- or grade- level group will process through the first chapter in the student books using the Explore, Discover, and Decide methodology of the *Be My Disciples* curriculum. The following is an overview of the faith concepts and Disciple Power virtue for each grade.

GRADE 1 Chapter 1: The Bible
The Bible, which is God's Word, is where we learn about God's love.
Disciple Power: faithful

GRADE 2 Chapter 1: The Bible
The Bible, which is the revealed and written Word of God, is made up of the Old and New Testaments; the Gospels tell us about Jesus.
Disciple Power: respect

GRADE 3 Chapter 1: God Speaks to Us
God's gift of faith helps us to know and believe in him; God speaks to us through the Bible and through the Church.
Disciple Power: love

GRADE 4 Chapter 1: God's Word to Us
The Holy Spirit inspired the human authors of the Bible, which is the inspired Word of God; the New Testament begins with the four Gospels.
Disciple Power: truthfulness

GRADE 5 Chapter 1: Speak, Lord
Divine Revelation is God making himself known and revealing his plan of creation and Salvation; God most fully reveals himself through his Son, Jesus.
Disciple Power: knowledge

GRADE 6 Chapter 1: The Gift of Faith
God placed in our hearts the desire to know, love, and serve him; Jesus invites us to have faith in God; the creeds express the Church's faith in God.
Disciple Power: perseverance in faith

LET'S TAKE A BREAK!

When the age- or grade- level groups have completed their work with the first chapter for the day, invite them to join together with all of the children in the program for refreshments and play time. (Note: Some groups may finish before others. To avoid distractions for the groups still meeting, if possible, set up the break time activities away from the meeting spaces.)

DISCOVER, Part Two

INTRODUCE

- Invite all of the children to gather in the large group meeting space with their learning groups.

- Direct their attention to the We Believe wall. Going from group to group, ask the participants to name things they learned in their first sessions about what Catholics believe.

- Write or have volunteers write responses on the wall.

TEACH, REINFORCE, CONNECT

- Tell the children that they are now going to meet again in their age- or grade-level groups to discover more about what we believe as Catholics.

- Invite the catechists to proceed with their children to their classrooms or meeting rooms.

- Allow the groups to meet for approximately 1 hour, 15 minutes.

AT A GLANCE PART TWO

Each age- or grade- level group will process through the second chapter in the student books. Here is an overview of the faith concepts and Disciple Power virtue for each grade.

GRADE 1 Chapter 2: God Loves Us
God's gift of faith helps us know and believe in him; Jesus shows us who God is.
Disciple Power: generosity

GRADE 2 Chapter 2: We Know and Love God
God reveals himself in creation; Jesus is the greatest sign of God's love.
Disciple Power: hospitality

GRADE 3 Chapter 2: God the Creator
God is the Creator; God created us in his image and likeness.
Disciple Power: generosity

GRADE 4 Chapter 2: I Will Be Your God
God gives us the gift of faith; God has revealed himself most fully in his Son, Jesus Christ.
Disciple Power: faith

GRADE 5 Chapter 2: The Word of God
The Bible is the inspired Word of God; the New Testament reveals that Jesus Christ is the new and everlasting Covenant.
Disciple Power: reverence

GRADE 6 Chapter 2: The Word of God
Through the Bible, God reveals himself and his loving plan of Salvation.
Disciple Power: knowledge

LET'S WRAP IT UP!

REINFORCE

- Gather the children and their catechists in the large group meeting space.

- Direct everyone's attention once again to the We Believe wall. Going from group to group, ask the participants to name things they learned in their second session about what Catholics believe.

- Write or have volunteers write responses on the newsprint.

- Summarize the learning for the large group.

- Collect the extra set of Faith Vocabulary/Faith Words cards that each group has made. Save these for Day 5.

WE REMEMBER

- Invite each group to present the one activity they have chosen to share from their chapters.

- Have each group present its Disciple Power virtue(s). As the groups present, post their Disciple Power words either around the room, or create a collage. You will add new Disciple Power words each day.

 If time permits, play a Jeopardy-style game, Name that Faith Word, using the Faith Vocabulary/Faith Words cards you have collected. (Note: Save all of the cards! You will continue to use them during the sessions.)

WE PRAY

- Choose the prayer from one of the grade level books from either Chapter 1 or Chapter 2 to pray together as a large group. Or use the following prayer ritual outlined on the following page.

- Gather the children in the prayer space, around the prayer table.

- Invite the children to quiet themselves, and to remember that God is with them in this time and place.

- Lead the children in praying the prayer you have chosen.

We Pray

• Light a candle, and place a Bible for each group next to the candle.

Briefly talk about light as a symbol of faith – Jesus is the Light of the world and he shows us the way to God. Light shows us the way in the darkness.

(If possible, project an image of light shining in the darkness on a screen or wall near the prayer space.)

• Within each small group, have the children pass a Bible from one person to the next, beginning with the catechist.

Tell the children that when it is their turn to hold the Bible, they are to say,

"God, I thank you for _____ who has helped teach me your way."

The rest of the children in the group will respond, **"Lord, help us know you and love you."**

Close with the following prayer:

Leader: God of truth,
help us find you in the Bible,
in the Church,
in creation,
and in other people.
Help us to always listen
when you speak.
We ask this through
Christ our Lord.
All: **Amen.**

TO TAKE HOME

Have the children take home the Chapter Review and With My Family page from Chapters 1 and 2 to share with their families.

Great is the Lord

"My soul proclaims the greatness of the Lord; my spirit rejoices in God my savior."

(Luke 1:46-47)

Background

Life is God's generous gift to humankind. The beauty of creation, the order of the universe, and the intricacies of all living things point to the wonder and greatness of God. God has come to us and comes to us now. He revealed himself and his loving plan of creation and Salvation to us.

Throughout Salvation History to this very day, people from all walks of life in all times and places praise the name of God. Mary, the Mother of God, proclaimed God's greatest in her song of praise when she said yes to God's invitation to be the mother of his Son, Jesus. You and the children, together with the whole Church, can join with Mary to magnify the Lord when you proclaim: "My soul proclaims the greatness of the Lord; my spirit rejoices in God my savior" (Luke 1:46-47). God's grace pulls us into the light and life of faith. We are empowered, or graced, to conform our lives to the will of God. Together the children will reflect on how they rejoice in the presence of our God and proclaim the greatness of the Lord by how they live as disciples of Jesus Christ.

In Today's Session ... In Chapters 3 and 4 student books, depending on their grade levels, the children will explore faith concepts such as: God the Father; God's creation of the world; the mystery of the Holy Trinity; and Mary's role in God's plan of Salvation. They will learn about Disciple Power virtues, explore ways people of faith have lived those virtues, and be challenged to make faith choices about ways they can be disciples of Jesus.

Faith Focus

- God reveals himself and his loving plan of creation and Redemption.

- As Jesus' disciples, we proclaim God's greatness when we say "yes" to God through our words and actions.

My Planning Notes
DAY 2

_____
_____
_____
_____
_____
_____
_____
_____
_____
_____

Getting Started

In Advance

☐ Check in with your catechists and learning group leaders.

- Review the day's schedule.

- Explain and assign responsibilities for the Welcome, Let's Take A Break, and Let's Wrap It Up activities and prayers.

- Address any age- or grade- level specific needs your catechists may have, including materials needed.

- Ask the catechists to choose with their children one activity from the day's chapters to present to the large group during Let's Wrap It Up. Remind them to choose a creative strategy for presenting the two Disciple Power virtues to the large group (see pages 20-21) and to leave time at the end of their second session to plan the presentation.

☐ Set up the large group meeting space.

☐ Post the *We Believe* wall in the large group gathering space.

☐ Have leaders cut out the Disciple Power words each group will learn (from Chapters 3 and 4) using colorful construction paper. You will post these during the Let's Wrap It Up segment to continue the creation of a Disciple Power collage.

☐ Ask leaders to make a set of Faith Vocabulary/Faith Words cards from the two chapters. You will use these cards during Day 5, and, if time permits, during the Let's Wrap It Up segment in today's session.

☐ Optional: Assign someone to be the photographer or videographer for the *Be My Disciples* Digital Scrapbook (see pages 18-19). Set up the digital scrapbook to be showing as the children enter the session.

Materials

☐ Bible, candle, cross, cloth for prayer space

☐ *Be My Disciples* student books

☐ Newsprint, markers, and tape

☐ Foam ball

☐ CD player and *Be My Disciples* Music CD

☐ Optional: projector, screen for Digital Scrapbook

WELCOME

Be on hand to greet the children when they arrive. This will help them feel safe and ready to learn. The Warm Up activity on Day 2 provides the opportunity for the children to continue to get to know each other and their catechists.

ICEBREAKER

- Invite all of the children to gather in the large meeting space.

- Play a large group icebreaker such as Toss the Ball. The large group can be in a circle, sitting together on the floor, or in chairs. Tell the children that you are going to toss the ball to one of them and, when catching it, that person calls out his or her name then immediately tosses it to someone else. That person calls out his or her name, tosses it to another participant, and so on. The goal is to ensure that everyone has been tossed the ball at least once. Then, try this variation. Have the person tossing the ball call out the name of the person catching the ball. Challenge the children to toss the ball to someone they don't know.

LET'S GET FOCUSED

- Invite the children to join their catechists in their age- or grade- level learning groups.

- In their groups, ask them to describe to each other how people generally react when something amazing, awesome, or wondrous happens to them. Then, have them choose one of these events, and quickly create an impromptu skit whereby they demonstrate their reaction to the situation.

- Invite the learning groups to share their improvisations. (You can also call out situations that are awesome and amazing, and ask the groups to react. For example, "Your team just won the Super Bowl!" "Your new baby sister or brother was just born." Or, have each learning group write down, on index cards, amazing, awesome, or wondrous events. Collect the cards, have each group draw one, and have volunteers act out their reactions to what is described on the cards.)

- Tell the children that something amazing and wondrous happened to Mary in the Gospels. Ask if they can recall the scene from the Gospels where the angel Gabriel appears to Mary.

- Have several volunteers tell or act out the story as they remember it.

- Have one of the group leaders read the Scripture story, Luke 1:26-37, as a lead-in to the prayer.

Bless Us, Lord

Ask the children to bow their heads, close their eyes for a brief moment, and remember that God is present with them in this time and place.

 Begin today's opening prayer with the song, "Here I Am Lord" from the *Be My Disciples* Music Program, Grade 3 and Grade 5 CDs.

• Begin prayer with the Sign of the Cross.

• Invite a child to read aloud Luke 1:46-47 from the Bible.

• Have volunteers name aloud reasons why they know that "God is great."

• End with the following prayer and the Sign of the Cross.

Lord God,
We ask for your blessing upon us.
Help us place our trust in you
as all of the people of faith
who have come before us
have done.
Help us see your greatness
and love in every moment
of our day.
May we always rejoice in
your presence in our lives.
Bless our time together today.
Amen.

DISCOVER, Part One

INTRODUCE

• Briefly describe the overall schedule for the day. Share any housekeeping information.

• Play a quick game of On the Spot to review learning from the previous day's lesson. In On the Spot, you call out characteristics of the participants and have those who share that characteristic stand up. These children are then On the Spot to name one learning from the previous day. For example, "Everyone with blue eyes, stand up." "Everyone who has an older brother or sister, stand up," and so forth.

• Point out the learning shared by the children that names what we believe as Catholics. Show the group the We Believe wall, and add any new words or phrases that may have arisen in the game.

AT A GLANCE PART ONE

Each age- or grade- level group will process through Chapter 3 in the student books using the Explore, Discover, and Decide methodology of the *Be My Disciples* curriculum. Here is an overview of the faith concepts and Disciple Power virtue for each grade. Groups will share about their Disciple Power virtues in the Let's Wrap It Up activity.

GRADE 1 Chapter 3: God, Our Father and Creator
God made the world out of love; we are created in God's image and likeness; Jesus taught us that God is our Father.
Disciple Power: wonder

GRADE 2 Chapter 3: The Holy Trinity
The Holy Trinity is God the Father, Jesus the Son, and the Holy Spirit.
Disciple Power: wonder

GRADE 3 Chapter 3: Mary Trusted God
God chose Mary to be the mother of his Son, Jesus; Jesus is the Son of God and the Son of Mary; Mary shows us what it means to say "Yes" to God.
Disciple Power: honor

GRADE 4 Chapter 3: The Mystery of God
God is the Almighty who is all-knowing, all-loving, truth, and faithfulness; God is the Creator and we are created in his image and likeness.
Disciple Power: trust

GRADE 5 Chapter 3: The Holy Trinity
The Holy Trinity is the central belief of the faith of the Church whose mystery is fully realized in Jesus Christ; we profess belief in the Holy Trinity when we say the Nicene Creed.
Disciple Power: wonder and awe

GRADE 6 Chapter 3: The Word of God
Creation is the work of the Holy Trinity; the mystery of the Holy Trinity is at the center of our faith.
Disciple Power: wonder and awe

TEACH, REINFORCE, CONNECT

- Tell the children that they are now going to meet in their age- or grade- level groups to discover more about what we believe as Catholics.

- Invite the catechists to gather their children, and proceed to their classrooms or meeting rooms.

- Allow groups to meet for approximately one hour.

LET'S TAKE A BREAK!

When the age- or grade-level groups have completed their work with the first chapter for the day, invite them to join together with all of the children in the program for refreshments and play time. (Note: Some groups may finish before others. To avoid distractions for the groups still meeting, if possible, set up the Let's Take A Break activities away from the meeting spaces.)

DISCOVER, Part Two

INTRODUCE

- Play Toss the Ball once again with the large group. This time, the person who receives the ball fills in the blank: "So far today I have learned _____."

- Add words and phrases to the We Believe wall based on what the children share.

TEACH, REINFORCE, CONNECT

- Tell the children that they are now going to meet again in their age- or grade- level groups.

- Invite the catechists to proceed with their children to their classrooms or meeting rooms.

- Allow groups to meet for approximately 1 hour, 15 minutes.

LET'S WRAP IT UP!

REINFORCE

- Invite all of the children to gather, with their catechists, in the main meeting space.

AT A GLANCE PART TWO

Each age- or grade- level group will process through Chapter 4 in the student books. Here is an overview of the faith concepts and Disciple Power virtue for each grade.

GRADE 1 Chapter 4: Jesus, the Son of God
Jesus is the Son of God and son of Mary who shared God's love with everyone. The family of Jesus, Mary, and Joseph is the Holy Family.
Disciple Power: kindness

GRADE 2 Chapter 4: God, Our Father
God is the Creator who is almighty and can do all things. Jesus taught us that God is our Father.
Disciple Power: honor

GRADE 3 Chapter 4: Jesus, the Son of God
Jesus is the Messiah, the Savior God promised to send. Jesus announced the Good News of God's kingdom.
Disciple Power: justice

GRADE 4 Chapter 4: God's Promise
God created us to be happy with him now and forever. God promised to send someone who would save all people from sin. Jesus is the Savior God promised.
Disciple Power: hope

GRADE 5 Chapter 4: Great is the Lord
God is one, almighty, holy, eternal, love and truth. God is the Creator. The sin of Adam and Eve was the beginning of sin in the world.
Disciple Power: joy

GRADE 6 Chapter 4: God, Father and Creator
God is Father, Creator of all things. Original Sin is the sin that Adam and Eve committed. In Jesus Christ we have been reconciled with one another and with all of creation.
Disciple Power: justice

- Direct everyone's attention once again to the We Believe wall. Going from group to group, ask the participants to name things they learned in their second session about what Catholics believe.

- Write or have volunteers write responses on the newsprint.

- Summarize the learning for the large group.

- Collect the extra set of Faith Vocabulary/Faith Words cards that each group has made. Save these for Day 5.

WE REMEMBER

- Invite each group to present the one activity they have chosen to share from their chapters.

- Have each group present its Disciple Power virtues. Continue making the Disciple Power collage by adding today's virtues to it.

- If time permits, play Name that Faith Word (see page 34).

WE PRAY

- Choose the prayer from one of the grade level books from either Chapter 3 or Chapter 4 to pray together as a large group. Or use the prayer outlined below.

- Invite the children to gather in the prayer space. Have everyone think about one way they have recently seen the greatness of the Lord, either at home, in school, at the parish, or in the neighborhood.

We Pray

Begin today's prayer with "Woman of God", from the *Be My Disciples* Music Program, Grade 1 and Grade 5 CDs.

- Light a candle and pray together the Sign of the Cross

Leader: *Ask the children to share with the people on either side of them one way they have seen the greatness of the Lord.*

Invite volunteers to share with the large group. After each person shares, together pray:

"O God, you are great indeed."

Leader: May we sing praise to God as Mary did.

(Have the children echo the following after you.)

All: "My soul proclaims the greatness of the Lord, my spirit rejoices in God my savior."

Leader: God of all goodness, we rejoice in your presence. May we experience the wonder and awe of your great love and your great works in our lives. We ask this through Christ our Lord.

All: Amen.

TO TAKE HOME

Remind the catechists and group leaders to have the children take home the Chapter Review and With My Family page from Chapters 3 and 4 to share with their families.

Jesus, the Messiah

"You are the Messiah, the Son of the living God."

(Matthew 16:16)

Background

The mystery of the Incarnation—the fact that the Son of God became human without giving up his divinity— reveals the infinite love of God for us. Jesus Christ is true God and true man. In him, God's promises are fulfilled. Jesus' whole life on Earth proclaimed God's love and care for us all.

For most of his life on Earth, Jesus was not a recognized public figure. He lived a life similar to that of most of his contemporaries and gave little evidence of his greatness. He lived in Nazareth, obeyed Mary and Joseph, and observed the laws and traditions of the Jewish religion. After John baptized Jesus in the Jordan River, Jesus began his public life and ministry.

Jesus once asked his disciples, "Who do you say that I am? (based on Matthew 16:15). Simon Peter answered: "'You are the Messiah, the Son of the living God"' (Matthew 16:16). All of Jesus the Messiah's deeds and words reveal God's saving love and invite us to follow him and become his disciples.

In Today's Session ... In Chapters 5 and 6 of each of the grade levels, the children will explore faith concepts such as: God chose Mary to be the mother of his Son; Jesus' birth is a sign of God's love and mercy; Jesus is the Savior God promised to send; Jesus is the Messiah and Second Person of the Holy Trinity; and the Paschal Mystery. They will learn about Disciple Power virtues, explore ways people of faith have lived the virtues, and be challenged to make faith choices about ways they can be disciples of Jesus.

Faith Focus

- Jesus is the Son of God, the Messiah.

- The Paschal Mystery is the mystery of Jesus' Passion, Death, Resurrection and Ascension

My Planning Notes
DAY 3

_____

_____

_____

_____

_____

_____

_____

_____

_____

Getting Started

In Advance

❑ Check in with your catechists and learning group leaders.

- Review the day's schedule.

- Explain and assign responsibilities as needed for the Welcome, Let's Take A Break, and Let's Wrap It Up activities and prayers.

- Address any age- or grade- level specific needs your catechists may have, including materials needed.

- Remind the catechists to choose with their children one activity from the day's chapters to present to the large group during Let's Wrap It Up. Remind them to choose a creative strategy for presenting the two Disciple Power virtues to the large group (see pages 20-21), and to leave a bit of time at the end of their second session to plan the presentation.

❑ Set up the large group meeting space. Post the We Believe wall.

❑ Prepare the prayer environment.

❑ Gather materials for large group activities.

❑ Have leaders cut out the Disciple Power words each group will learn (from Chapters 5 and 6) using colorful construction paper. You will post these during the Let's Wrap It Up segment to continue the creation of a Disciple Power collage.

❑ Ask leaders to make a set of Faith Vocabulary/Faith Words cards from the two chapters. You will use these cards during Day 5, and, if time permits, during the Let's Wrap It Up segment in today's session.

Materials

- ❑ Bible, candle, cross, cloth for prayer space
- ❑ *Be My Disciples* student books
- ❑ Newsprint, markers, and tape
- ❑ Sets of Barn Yard Animal cards for Icebreaker
- ❑ Several sets of alphabet cards, shuffled, for Jesus Scrabble (see Let's Get Focused)
- ❑ Religious objects such as crosses, one for each learning group
- ❑ CD player and *Be My Disciples* Music CD

WELCOME

You and the catechists should be on hand to greet the children when they arrive. This will help them feel safe and ready to learn.

ICEBREAKER

- Invite all of the children to gather in the large meeting space.

- Do a large group icebreaker, such as Barn Yard Animals, in order to divide the large group into smaller groups. For this game, distribute one of the animal cards to each person. On your "go", have the children imitate the sound of the animal on their cards. Tell them to find the other animals like theirs, and to form a group. Then have a Barn Yard Animal contest by asking each group to imitate its animal (sounds, motion, etc.) for the large group. See if the participants can agree on which group gave the most "authentic" imitation.

LET'S GET FOCUSED

Ask for the children's attention as you describe the next activity. Distribute a random set of alphabet cards to each group and introduce Jesus Scrabble.

- Using only its alphabet cards, each group is to come up with words that fill in the blank: "Jesus is _____." Give the groups a set amount of time to form the words.

- Invite the children to re-gather as a large group. Write "Jesus is" in the middle of a large sheet of newsprint. Have each group come forward and write the words they created on the newsprint. (Invite the children to share how easy or hard it was to form words from the cards they were dealt.)

- Talk briefly about their responses and then share the following: We believe that Jesus is the Son of God. Ask a volunteer to add that sentence to the We Believe wall. Tape the "Jesus is" newsprint to the We Believe wall while the children gather for opening prayer.

Bless Us, Lord

- Ask the children to bow their heads, close their eyes for a brief moment, and remember that God is present with them in this time and place.

- Begin by praying together the Sign of the Cross.

- Invite a volunteer to read aloud Matthew 16:15-16 from the Bible.

- Pose the question: How would you respond to Jesus' question, "Who do you say that I am?"

 Play "Open My Eyes" from the *Be My Disciples* Music Program, Grade 1 and Grade 6 CDs, while the participants reflect on the question.

- End with the following prayer, and the Sign of the Cross.

God the Father of all,

bless us as we learn

about your Son,

sign of your love and mercy,

Son of Mary,

the Christ, the Messiah,

and Lord.

Amen.

DISCOVER, Part One

INTRODUCE

- Briefly describe the overall schedule for the day. Share any housekeeping information.

- Point out the We Believe wall and the "Jesus is _____" newsprint. Tell the children that today they will learn more about what we believe about who Jesus is.

AT A GLANCE PART ONE

Each age- or grade- level group will process through Chapter 5 in the student books using the Explore, Discover, and Decide methodology of the *Be My Disciples* curriculum. Here is an overview of the faith concepts and Disciple Power virtue for each grade. Groups will share a creative presentation of their Disciple Power virtues in the Let's Wrap It Up activity.

GRADE 1 Chapter 5: Mary, the Mother of Jesus
God chose Mary to be the Mother of Jesus; Mary loves and trusts God.
Disciple Power: courage

GRADE 2 Chapter 5: Jesus, the Son of God
The Covenant is a sign of God's love and mercy; the birth of Jesus, the Son of God, is a sign of God's love and mercy.
Disciple Power: mercy

GRADE 3 Chapter 5: Jesus is Risen!
Jesus suffered and died on the Cross to save all people; Jesus rose from the dead.
Disciple Power: hope

GRADE 4 Chapter 5: The Son of God
Jesus is the only Son of God; everything Jesus did was a sign of God's love for people.
Disciple Power: love

GRADE 5 Chapter 5: Jesus Christ, Son of God
Jesus is the Christ, the Messiah; Jesus is Lord, true God, the Second Person of the Holy Trinity; Mary is the Mother of the Church.
Disciple Power: faithfulness

GRADE 6 Chapter 5: Son of God, Son of Mary
Jesus is the Messiah; God the Father chose Mary to be the mother of his Son.
Disciple Power: humility

TEACH, REINFORCE, CONNECT

- Tell the children that they are now going to meet in their age- or grade- level groups to discover more about what we believe as Catholics.

- Invite the catechists to gather their children, and proceed to their classrooms or meeting rooms.

- Allow groups to meet for approximately one hour.

LET'S TAKE A BREAK!

When the age- or grade- level groups have completed their work with the first chapter for the day, invite them to join together with all of the children in the program for refreshments and play time. (Note: Some groups may finish before others. To avoid distractions for the groups still meeting, if possible, set up the Let's Take a Break activities away from the meeting spaces.)

DISCOVER, Part Two

INTRODUCE

- Invite all of the children to gather in the large group meeting space with their learning groups.

- Direct their attention to the We Believe wall. Going from group to group, ask the participants to name things they learned in the day's first session about what Catholics believe.

- Write or have volunteers write responses on the newsprint.

TEACH, REINFORCE, CONNECT

- Tell the children that they are now going to meet again in their age- or grade-level groups to discover more about what we believe as Catholics.

- Invite the catechists to proceed with their children to their classrooms or meeting rooms.

AT A GLANCE PART TWO

Each age- or grade- level group will process through the second chapter in the student books. Here is an overview of the faith concepts and Disciple Power virtue for each grade.

GRADE 1 Chapter 6: Jesus Shares God's Love
Jesus loved us so much that he gave his life for us; Jesus died on the Cross and rose from the dead and is alive.
Disciple Power: hope

GRADE 2 Chapter 6: Jesus is the Savior
Jesus suffered death on the Cross to save all people; God the Father raised his Son, Jesus, from death to new life.
Disciple Power: sacrifice

GRADE 3 Chapter 6: The Gift of the Holy Spirit
God the Father sent the Holy Spirit to be with the Church; the Holy Spirit came to the disciples and helped them teach about Jesus.
Disciple Power: joy

GRADE 4 Chapter 6: The Death and Resurrection of Jesus
Jesus celebrated the Last Supper; Jesus suffered and died on the Cross for us; Jesus was raised from the dead and ascended to his Father in Heaven.
Disciple Power: courage

GRADE 5 Chapter 6: The Paschal Mystery
The Passover; by his Paschal Mystery Christ freed people from sin and death, gaining for all the promise and hope of eternal life.
Disciple Power: hope

GRADE 6 Chapter 6: The Suffering Servant
The Paschal Mystery; Jesus Christ suffered death for the Redemption and Salvation of humanity.
Disciple Power: mercy

LET'S WRAP IT UP!

REINFORCE

- Invite all of the children, with their catechists, to gather in the main meeting space.

- Have them play Barn Yard Animals again to regroup. Ask the older children in each of the groups to facilitate a small group discussion about what everyone in the group learned today.

- Direct everyone's attention to the We Believe wall. Going from group to group, ask the participants to name things they learned in their second session.

- Write or have volunteers write responses on the newsprint.

- Summarize the learning for the large group.

- Collect the extra set of Faith Vocabulary/Faith Words cards that each group has made. Save these for Day 5.

WE REMEMBER

- Have the learning groups present the one activity they have chosen to share.

- Have each group present its Disciple Power virtues. Continue making the Disciple Power collage by adding today's virtues to it.

- If time permits, play Name that Faith Word (see page 34).

WE PRAY

- Choose the prayer from one of the grade level books from Chapter 5 or Chapter 6 to pray together as a large group. Or use the following prayer.

- If using the following, have participants sit in their learning groups. Each group will need a religious object, such as a cross, to use during the prayer.

We Pray

Light a candle and pray together the Sign of the Cross.

Invite one person in each learning group to hold his or her group's religious object, and to pray for a member of his or her family, saying: **God, I am thankful for _____ because _____.**

The learning group members should respond together: **Help us to follow Jesus. Help our families be holy families.**

Repeat until all learning group members have offered the prayer.

 Play "A Faith-filled Heart" from the *Be My Disciples* Music Program, Grades 1, 3, and 5 CDs, while the small groups pray.

Conclude by praying together the Sign of the Cross.

 ## TO TAKE HOME

Remind the catechists and group leaders to have the children take home the Chapter Review and With My Family page from Chapters 5 and 6 to share with their families.

Go and Make Disciples

"Go, therefore, and make disciples of all nations, baptizing them in the name of the Father, and of the Son, and of the holy Spirit, teaching them to observe all that I have commanded you. And behold, I am with you always, until the end of the age."

(Matthew 28:19-20)

Background

The Church is the People of God and the Body of Christ. The Church is the Communion of Saints—the faithful alive on Earth and the faithful who have died, the community of followers of Jesus who are in relationship with one another.

Today's Scripture passage, Matthew 28: 19-20, reminds us that we, the Church, are called to make Christ visible, to continue his mission, and to be signs of Christ in the world. Through the community of the Church our faith is nurtured and flourishes.

In Today's Session … In Chapters 7 and 8 of each of their grade levels, the children will learn that the Holy Spirit and the Church help us do what Jesus taught; the Saints help us live as Jesus' followers; the Church is the People of God, Communion of Saints, and Body of Christ; Jesus founded the Church on Saint Peter the Apostle; Jesus announced the coming of the Kingdom of God; the Church is one, holy, catholic, and apostolic; and Jesus Christ is the Head of the Church. They will learn about Disciple Power virtues, explore ways people of faith have lived those virtues, and be challenged to make faith choices about ways they can be disciples of Jesus. During today's session, they will reflect on Jesus' words, "Go make disciples…" (Matthew 28:19).

Faith Focus

- Jesus promised that God the Father and he would send the Holy Spirit.

- The Church is the People of God.

- We belong to the Catholic Church. The Church lives out the command of Jesus to "Go make disciples."

My Planning Notes DAY 4

_____
_____
_____
_____
_____
_____
_____
_____
_____
_____

Getting Started

In Advance

☐ Check in with your catechists and learning group leaders.

- Review the day's schedule.

- Explain and assign responsibilities as needed for the Welcome, Let's Take A Break, and Let's Wrap It Up activities and prayers.

- Address any age- or grade- level specific needs your catechists may have, including materials needed.

- Remind the catechists to choose with their children one activity from the day's chapters to present to the large group during Let's Wrap It Up. Remind them to choose a creative strategy for presenting the two Disciple Power virtues to the large group (see pages 20-21), and to leave a bit of time at the end of their second session to plan the presentation.

☐ Have leaders cut out the Disciple Power words each group will learn (from Chapters 7 and 8) using colorful construction paper. You will post these during the Let's Wrap It Up segment to continue the creation of a Disciple Power collage.

☐ Ask leaders to make a set of Faith Vocabulary/Faith Words cards from the two chapters. You will use these cards during Day 5, and, if time permits, during the Let's Wrap It Up segment in today's session.

☐ Optional: Assign someone to be the photographer or videographer for the *Be My Disciples* Digital Scrapbook (see pages 18-19). Set up the digital scrapbook to be showing as the children enter the session.

Materials

☐ Bible, candle, cross, cloth for prayer space

☐ *Be My Disciples* student books

☐ CD player and *Be My Disciples* Music CD

☐ Optional: projector, screen for Digital Scrapbook

WELCOME

You and the catechists should be on hand to greet them children when they arrive. This will help them feel safe and ready to learn.

ICEBREAKER

- Invite all of the children to gather in the large meeting space.

- Number off the group to form small groups of six to ten participants. Assign one or more leaders to each group to help facilitate the activity.

- Have each small group create a machine with moving parts, using their bodies. Each part of the body must have a functioning purpose to the machine.

- Invite each of the groups to present their machines to the large group.

LET'S GET FOCUSED

- Facilitate a large group discussion about the activity. Ask questions such as: What was difficult about creating your machine? How easy or difficult was it to ensure each member of your group was part of the machine? How would your machine have been different if you had fewer or more people to build it? What do you think is the most important thing you can learn from this activity?

- Tell the children that one of the most important aspects of the activity was that everyone in the group was an important part of the machine. If one person "broke down", the machine would not work. Suggest that, as members of the Body of Christ, we are each important to the Church. Ask: What do you think it means to be the Body of Christ?

- Optional activity if time permits: Have the children gather with their learning groups. Give each group a piece of newsprint and markers. Have the groups work together to draw a church. Encourage them to illustrate their churches by adding signs or symbols inside or around the church that represent what the church is or what the word "church" means to them. Have each group share its drawing. The participants' general understanding of "Church" will surface from this activity.

©2013 RCL Publishing LLC

Bless Us, Lord

- Ask the children to bow their heads, close their eyes for a brief moment, and remember that God is present with them in this time and place.

- Begin prayer by praying together the Sign of the Cross.

- Invite a child to read aloud Matthew 28:19-20 from the Bible.

- Pose the question: What are the ways that other people know that we are disciples of Jesus? Have the children share with a partner.

🎵 Sing together "We Are Disciples" from the *Be My Disciples* Music Program. It appears on each grade level CD.

- End with the prayer, followed by the Sign of the Cross.

God of all people, bless us and be with us as we learn how to live as the Body of Christ. Amen.

DISCOVER, Part One

INTRODUCE

- Briefly decribe the overall schedule for the day. Share any housekeeping information.

- Point out the We Believe wall. Have the catechists or learning group leaders name one or two things that their groups will discover today about the Church.

AT A GLANCE PART ONE

Each age- or grade- level group will process through Chapter 7 in the student books using the Explore, Discover, and Decide methodology of the *Be My Disciples* curriculum. Here is an overview of the faith concepts and Disciple Power virtue for each grade. Groups will share a creative presentation of their Disciple Power virtues in the large group Let's Wrap It Up activity.

GRADE 1 Chapter 7: The Holy Spirit, Our Helper
The Holy Spirit helps and teaches us to pray and gives us gifts; the Holy Trinity is One God in Three Divine Persons.
Disciple Power: counsel

GRADE 2 Chapter 7: The Holy Spirit
Jesus promised the Father would send the Holy Spirit; the Holy Spirit came to the disciples on Pentecost.
Disciple Power: generosity

GRADE 3 Chapter 7: The Church
The Church is the holy People of God; all the people of the Church are called to live holy lives and help others know and follow Jesus.
Disciple Power: faithfulness

GRADE 4 Chapter 7: Receive the Holy Spirit
Jesus promised that he and the Father would send the Holy Spirit; the Holy Spirit came on Pentecost; the work of the Holy Spirit in the Church continues the work the Father sent Jesus to do.
Disciple Power: wisdom

GRADE 5 Chapter 7: Many Gifts, One Spirit
Jesus sent the Holy Spirit to guide the Church as her advocate, teacher, and sanctifier; the Holy Spirit makes the Church holy.
Disciple Power: courage

GRADE 6 Chapter 7: The Holy Spirit
The Holy Spirit is at work bringing about God's plan of Salvation and strengthening the Church to be a sign of Christ's love; the Gifts of the Holy Spirit help us continue the mission of the Church.
Disciple Power: counsel

TEACH, REINFORCE, CONNECT

- Tell the children that they are now going to meet in their age- or grade-level groups to discover more about what we believe as Catholics.
- Invite the catechists to gather their children, and proceed to their classrooms or meeting rooms.
- Allow groups to meet for approximately one hour.

LET'S TAKE A BREAK!

When the age- or grade- level groups have completed their work with the first chapter for the day, invite them to join together with all of the children in the program for refreshments and play time. (Note: Some groups may finish before others. To avoid distractions for the groups still meeting, if possible, set up the Break Time activities away from the meeting spaces.)

DISCOVER, Part Two

INTRODUCE

- Invite all of the children to gather in the large group meeting space with their learning groups.
- Direct their attention to the We Believe wall. Going from group to group, ask the participants to name things they learned in the day's first session about what Catholics believe.
- Write or have volunteers write responses on the newsprint.

TEACH, REINFORCE, CONNECT

- Tell the children that they are now going to meet again in their age- or grade- level groups.
- Invite the catechists to proceed with their children to their classrooms or meeting rooms.
- Allow groups to meet for approximately 1 hour, 15 minutes.

AT A GLANCE PART TWO

Each age- or grade- level group will process through Chapter 8 in the student books. Here is an overview of the faith concepts and Disciple Power virtue for each grade.

GRADE 1 Chapter 8: The Church
The Holy Spirit helps all members of the Church; the Church helps us do what Jesus taught; the Saints help us live as followers of Jesus.
Disciple Power: reverence

GRADE 2 Chapter 8: The Church
The Church is the People of God who follow Jesus; the Church is the Body of Christ and the Communion of Saints.
Disciple Power: goodness

GRADE 3 Chapter 8: The Communion of Saints
The Church is the Body of Christ and the Communion of Saints; Saints are those people whose love for God is stronger than their love for anything or anyone else.
Disciple Power: humility

GRADE 4 Chapter 8: The People of God
The Church is the Body of Christ, the People of God, and the Communion of Saints; Jesus founded the Church on Saint Peter the Apostle; Jesus announced the Kingdom of God.
Disciple Power: understanding

GRADE 5 Chapter 8: Thy Kingdom Come
The Church is made up of the lay faithful, the ordained, and members of the consecrated life; the Church has four Marks; members of the Church work together for the coming of the Kingdom of God.
Disciple Power: peace

GRADE 6 Chapter 8: The Mystery of the Church
Jesus Christ is the Head of the Church; the Holy Spirit strengthens the Church to be one, holy, catholic, and apostolic; the Kingdom of God is present in the Church and will come about in the fullness of time.
Disciple Power: peace

LET'S WRAP IT UP!

REINFORCE

- Invite all of the children to gather, with their catechists, in the main meeting space.
- Direct everyone's attention to the We Believe wall. Going from group to group, ask the participants to name things they learned in their second session.
- Write or have volunteers write responses on the newsprint.
- Summarize the learning for the large group.
- Collect the extra set of Faith Vocabulary/Faith Words cards that each group has made. Save these for Day 5.

WE REMEMBER

- Invite each group to present the one activity they have chosen to share from their chapters.
- Have each group present its Disciple Power virtues. Continue making the Disciple Power collage by adding today's virtues to it.
- If time permits, play Name that Faith Word (see page 34).

WE PRAY

- Choose the prayer from Chapter 7 or Chapter 8, or use the following prayer.
- Have the children form circles in their learning groups around the prayer table.

We Pray

- Light a candle and pray together the Sign of the Cross.
- Reader: Read aloud Matthew 29: 19-20.
- Leader: Ask each person to stand in the center of his or her circle.

Invite the other members of the group to say together:

Lord, help _____ go and make disciples by living as a disciple of Jesus.

Ask the person in the circle to respond:

I will go and make disciples by the witness of my life.

 When all of the groups are finished, conclude by singing together "We Are Disciples" from the *Be My Disciples* Music Program (all CDs).

 ## TO TAKE HOME

Remind the catechists and group leaders to have the children take home the Chapter Review and With My Family page from Chapters 7 and 8 to share with their families.

I Believe!

"Jesus came, . . . stood in their midst and said, "Peace be with you." Then he said to Thomas, "Put your finger here and see my hands, and bring your hand and put it into my side and do not be unbelieving, but believe." Thomas answered and said to him, "My Lord and my God!" Jesus said to him, "Have you come to believe because you have seen me? Blessed are those who have not seen and have believed." These [signs] are written that you may [come to] believe that Jesus is the Messiah, the Son of God, and that through this belief you may have life in his name."

(John 20:26-31)

Background

The quest for God is imprinted on our hearts. This is understandable, considering that God created us and planted within us something like a homing device that compels us to seek him. Saint Augustine of Hippo has this to say about our quest for God: "[Y]ou have made us for yourself, and our hearts are restless until they rest in you" (Confessions 1).

During the past few days, the children have learned that they are loved by God and, as his adopted daughters and sons, they are alive in his grace. They have learned that God invites us to freely accept his gift of faith and to respond to him.

Faith is not simply believing in something—the truth that God has revealed. Faith is believing in Someone—God, who reveals the truth of his love. Walking by faith means seeing God's truth unfold in the events of daily life and placing ourselves continually in his hands.

While living a life of faith is deeply personal, it is not a private, solitary pursuit. God the Father sends us the Holy Spirit and has established the Church in Christ to assist us in responding to him and living a life of faith.

In Today's Session ... Today's session gives the children the opportunity to enrich their learning of the past week and to deepen their understanding of the concepts they have explored regarding what we believe as Catholics. The Activity Center experiences that you and the catechists create will reinforce what the children have learned in Chapters 1 – 8, Catholic Social Teaching, and Liturgical Year lessons. At the end of this session, they will showcase their work in an Interactive Gallery.

My Planning Notes
DAY 5

_____
_____
_____
_____
_____
_____
_____
_____
_____
_____

AT A GLANCE DAY 5 CHAPTERS 1 - 8

Enriching the Lesson Activities	Chapter 1, page 55	Chapter 2, page 67	Chapter 3, page 79	Chapter 4, page 91	Chapter 5, page 107	Chapter 6, page 119	Chapter 7, page 131	Chapter 8, page 143
Grade 1	□ Retelling Bible Stories □ Telephone Game □ Literature Connection	□ Who Am I? □ Learning from Our Families □ Literature Connection	□ Making a Creation Book □ Taking a Creation Walk □ Literature Connection	□ Creating a Chain of Kindness □ Literature Connection	□ Creating Bookmarks of Faith □ Bible Story Puppets □ Listening Carefully	□ Making Crosses □ Retelling Scripture Stories □ Literature Connection	□ Making a Collage □ Creating a Symbol for the Holy Spirit □ Literature Connection	□ Sequencing the Story of Pentecost □ Making a Word Search
Grade 2	□ The Listener Game □ Proclaiming God's Word □ Literature Connection	□ Making Creation Posters □ Taking the Scriptures Outdoors □ Literature Connection	□ Illustrating the Holy Trinity □ Role-playing Living as Children of God □ Celebrating the Trinity with Music	□ Using Gestures in Storytelling □ Literature Connection	□ Pantomiming a Scripture Story □ Making Headlines □ Literature Connection	□ Making Story Cards □ Designing a Parish Bulletin Board □ Literature Connection	□ Making a Holy Spirit Display □ Making a Holy Spirit Collage □ Literature Connection	□ Acting Out Scripture Stories □ Literature Connection
Grade 3	□ Creating Bookmarks □ Honoring God's Word □ Living Our Faith	□ Creating a Baruch Tableau □ Designing Messenger of Hope Murals □ Using Time Lines	□ Writing Acrostic Poems □ Creating Paper Mosaics □ Literature Connection	□ Writing Diamantes □ Creating a Scripture Service	□ Role-playing Saying "Yes" to God □ Designing Symbols for Mary □ Writing in Journals	□ Developing a TV Episode □ Designing Crosses □ Expressing Faith through Art	□ Decoding a Gospel Message □ Celebrating the Holy Spirit □ Portraying the Holy Spirit	□ Sharing Faith □ Role-playing a Journey
Grade 4	□ Character Maps: Biblical Figures □ Decoding Bible Verses □ Making a Word Search	□ Role-play: Trusting Others □ Collage: Living Our Faith □ Pantomime: Living Our Faith	□ Photo Book on Creation □ Trust Walk □ Public Service Announcement	□ Designing a Personal Emblem □ Making Messiah Bookmarks	□ Drawing Activity on Following Jesus □ Creating Games to Review Faith Vocabulary □ Creating a Refrain about God's Love	□ Making Crosses □ Play: Jesus' Last Day on Earth □ Putting Events in Order	□ Interview: Questions for Jesus □ Reports: They Have the Holy Spirit □ Role Play: Be an Advocate	□ Chain-Reaction Pantomime □ Singing about the Kingdom
Grade 5	□ Designing Wonders of Creation Album of Songs □ Creating a Making a Difference Bulletin Board □ Creating a Word Web	□ Using Drama Overcoming Fears □ Creating a Bible App	□ Making Holy Trinity Posters □ Imagining the Council of Nicaea □ Role-playing the Story about Saint Augustine	□ Affirming One Another □ Making a Prayer Booklet	□ Making Acrostics □ Making Bookmarks □ Creating a Time Line	□ Reflections on the Stations of the Cross □ Exploring the Passover □ Creating Paschal Mystery Dioramas	□ Asking Jesus Questions □ Developing Character Maps □ Making a Courage Collage	□ Creating Word Puzzles □ Identifying Faith-filled People
Grade 6	□ Creating Bookmarks □ Honoring God's Word □ Living Our Faith	□ Creating a Baruch Tableau □ Designing a Messenger of Hope Mural □ Using Time Lines	□ Writing Acrostic Poems □ Creating Paper Mosaics □ Literature Connection	□ Writing Diamantes □ Creating a Scripture Service	□ Role-playing Saying "Yes" to God □ Designing Symbols for Mary □ Writing in Journals	□ Developing a TV Episode □ Designing Crosses □ Expressing Faith through Art	□ Decoding a Gospel Message □ Celebrating the Holy Spirit □ Portraying the Life of the Holy Spirit	□ Sharing Faith □ Role-playing a Journey

Getting Started

In Advance

❑ Schedule a time with your catechists to plan for this session. On Day 5 the children will participate in hands-on, interactive learning activities focused around their chapter learning, Catholic Social Teaching, and Liturgical Year lessons.

❑ If you have chosen the Friday afternoon/ evening option for Days 5, 10, and 15 with a potluck community meal, send out reminders to the families and larger community with details about the time, the place, and the meal.

❑ Determine the Activity Center format. You can plan grade- level activities using the smaller meeting spaces for each grade, or you can organize the large group meeting space as a Learning Center where the children rotate in small groups from one activity to the next.

AT A GLANCE	CATHOLIC SOCIAL TEACHING	
Catholic Social Teaching Activities	Unit One, page 91	Unit Two, page 143
Grade 1	❑ Making Bird Feeders	❑ Letters about Hunger
Grade 2	❑ Choosing a Nature Project	❑ Creating a Mural
Grade 3	❑ Our Stewardship Process	❑ Kingdom of God Triptych
Grade 4	❑ Planning a Project for Needy People	❑ People of God Posters
Grade 5	❑ Preserving God's Gift of Water	❑ Making Get Well Cards
Grade 6	❑ Charting Our Stewardship Process	❑ Kingdom of God Triptych

❑ Determine the number of activities and leadership you will need for today's session.

• The number of activities you choose will depend on the number of participants in your program, and the leadership available to facilitate the activities. Ask young people from the parish's junior high and high school youth ministries to help set up and facilitate the day's activities.

• Organize the activities by age- or grade- level, or, by age- level groupings (primary, intermediate, or older children). Catechists from several grades can work together. You can plan a mix of age-specific and multi-age activities.

❑ Determine which learning activities will be a part of the interactive learning center. Refer to the grids on pages 55 and 56 for an overview of the many activities to choose from.

• Plan enough activities to fill two 1-hour time frames. Choose activities best suited for your group. Some are suitable for all grade levels, some work for age- level groups, and others would work nicely with older children helping the younger children. The Enriching the Lesson, Catholic Social Teaching, and Liturgical Year activities work well as presented in the Catechist Guides, but the catechists can also use them as a starting point for their own creativity. Adapt and revise activities to meet the needs of the group.

- The key is to aim for variety, creativity, and a bit of fun. Include a mix of Language and Music-related activities, person-related activities, and object-related activities. For more information and examples of each type, refer to 8 Kinds of Smart on page 27 in the Catechist Guide, and Activity Ideas on pages 18-19 of this manual. With your catechists, review and choose from the following:

Enriching the Lesson. Choose from the activities that appear at the end of Chapters 1 through 8 in the Catechist Guides, or create and plan similar types of activities. (See a complete listing of the activities for Chapters 1 - 8 on page 55.)

Catholic Social Teaching. Choose from activities that appear on page 91 (Unit 1: Care for God's Creation), and page 143 (Unit 2: Call to Family, Community, and Participation) in the Catechist Guides (see a listing on page 56).

The Liturgical Year. All Saints; Advent; Our Lady of Guadalupe; Christmas; Mary, Mother of God; and Epiphany. Choose from the lessons that appear on pages 358-371 in the Catechist Guides.

- ❏ Decide how the children will process through the activities. Will you form small age- or grade- level groups that will travel together through the activities? Will you allow the children to choose from among the activities?

- ❏ Set up the large group meeting space. For the icebreaker Tic Tac Toe game, use masking tape to create a tic tac toe board at least 6 ft. by 6 ft. in size. Write X's on sheets of construction paper and O's on additional sheets.

- ❏ Set up the Interactive Gallery or showcase space where the children will display their work (arts and crafts, worksheets, etc.), and where they will present role-plays, puppet shows, stories, or skits.

- ❏ Prepare the prayer environment. Today's opening prayer includes a dramatic presentation of John 20: 24-29. Invite volunteers to prepare the Scripture reading enactment by taking the parts of the narrator, Jesus, Thomas, and several disciples.

- ❏ Gather materials for all of the activities.

- ❏ Be sure you have one set of Faith Vocabulary/Faith Words cards from each age- or grade- level group for the eight chapters. You will use these in the Get Focused activity.

- ❏ Post the We Believe wall in the large group meeting space where all can see it. In addition, display the Disciple Power collage.

- ❏ Optional: Assign someone to be the photographer or videographer for the *Be My Disciples* Digital Scrapbook (see pages 18-19). Set up the digital scrapbook to be showing as the children enter the session.

WELCOME

You and the catechists should be on hand to greet the children when they arrive. This will help them feel safe and ready to participate.

ICEBREAKER

• Invite all of the children to gather in the large group meeting space.

• Play a large group icebreaker, Tic Tac Toe. Divide the participants into multiple teams. For the first round, one team is the X team, one team is the O team. Give each team three X or O papers. Alternately ask members of each team a level-appropriate question from the material covered during the We Believe week. When a team member answers a question correctly, he or she chooses a place to stand on the tic tac toe board (see In Advance) holding either an X or O paper. Continue with questions until one team gets three Xs or three O's in a row. Then, repeat the game giving the other teams a chance to play.

LET'S GET FOCUSED

• Using the set of Faith Vocabulary/Faith Words cards you have collected from each of the age- or grade- level groups, play a Jeopardy-style game. Draw a card, and read aloud the definition of the word that appears on one side of it. Volunteers can call out the correct word that corresponds to the definition. For example: "A gift from God that helps us believe in God and all that he has revealed." Response: "What is faith?" Be sure to call on both younger and older children.

• Call out some of the Disciple Power virtues that the children explored during the first four sessions. Have them offer examples of concrete ways they have practiced the virtues.

• Tell the children that the theme of this session is "I believe." Give them a moment to think about what they believe about God, and why. Ask, "What are some of the signs around us that show us that God exists?" Invite several volunteers to share with the large group.

• Transition into the opening prayer.

Materials

❑ Bible, candle, cross for prayer space

❑ Materials for activities in the Learning Center

❑ CD player and Be My Disciples Music CD

❑ Optional: projector, screen for Digital Scrapbook

©2013 RCL Publishing LLC

- Ask the children to bow their heads, close their eyes for a brief moment, and remember that God is present with them in this time and place.

 Begin and end today's prayer with the theme song, "We Are Disciples," from the *Be My Disciples* Music CD (all grade levels).

- Pray together the Sign of the Cross.

- Invite the volunteers you have chosen to present their reading/enactment of John 20: 24-31.

- Pose the question: In what ways do your words and actions show that you believe in Jesus Christ?

- End with the prayer, followed by the Sign of the Cross. The response is **"I believe!"**

Bless Us, Lord

Leader: I believe in one God, the Father almighty, maker of heaven and earth, of all things visible and invisible.
All: I believe!

Leader: I believe in one Lord Jesus Christ, the Only Begotten Son of God, born of the Father before all ages.
All: I believe!

Leader: I believe in the Holy Spirit, the Lord, the giver of life. With the Father and the Son he is adored and glorified.
All: I believe!

Leader: I believe in one, holy, catholic and apostolic Church.
All: I believe!

Leader: I confess one Baptism for the forgiveness of sins and I look forward to the resurrection of the dead and the life of the world to come. Amen.
All: I believe!

DISCOVER, Part One

INTRODUCE

- Briefly review some of the major faith concepts that appear on the We Believe wall. Tell the children that today they will have the opportunity to express what they have learned thus far in art, crafts, storytelling, and other creative activities.

- Provide a brief orientation for the session. Describe the various learning activities and how the children will process through them. Tell them about the Interactive Gallery where they will gather as a large group at the end of the session to share their work.

TEACH, REINFORCE, CONNECT

- Invite the children to join their learning groups. Their catechists and leaders will be their guides as they travel through the activity stations.

- Allow approximately one hour for the children to visit the activity stations.

- Have the children bring the art, crafts, worksheets, etc. that they worked on during the first part of the session to their grades' section of the Interactive Gallery before moving into the break.

LET'S TAKE A BREAK!

Invite the children to join together for refreshments and play time. (Note: Some groups may finish before others. To avoid distractions for the groups still working on their activities, if possible, set up the Let's Take A Break activities away from the meeting spaces.)

DISCOVER, Part Two

INTRODUCE

- Invite all of the children back into the large group meeting space. Have the children quietly file past the We Believe wall. Then, ask them which items on the wall they have focused on in their activities thus far today.

- Tell the children that they are going to continue with several more activities, and then design their section of the Interactive Gallery.

TEACH, REINFORCE, CONNECT

- Invite the catechists and leaders to continue facilitating the activity centers.

- Allow the groups to complete one or more activities, and then direct them to display their arts, crafts, worksheets, etc. in the Interactive Gallery space.

LET'S WRAP IT UP!

REINFORCE

- Have the children gather together in the Interactive Gallery space.

- Give them time to file through the gallery and view the things displayed there.

- Have them sign their names on the We Believe wall.

WE REMEMBER

- Invite children and their catechists to briefly explain their work.

- Have the groups who have something to present do so (such as skits, role-plays, songs, poems, storytelling, puppet shows, etc.)

WE PRAY

- Have the children gather together in the prayer space.

- Invite everyone to think about a person who has helped them believe in God.

We Pray

 Play the instrumental, "A Faith-Filled Heart" from the *Be My Disciples* Music Program, Grades 1, 3, and 6 CDs.

- Invite the same group who presented John 20: 24-31 to re-present the Scripture story.

- Repeat the I Believe prayer from the session's opening prayer. This time consider assigning the Leader parts to volunteers.

- Invite participants to share a Sign of Peace.

Invite the Community

Optional: Share a potluck lunch or dinner with the children and their families to end the first week of the program.

Consider inviting members of the parish community to join you today for all or part of the session. They could be a part of the learning activities with the children, come for the Interactive Gallery and presentations, and join the children in prayer and celebration (i.e., potluck meal).

Be My Disciples Week Two Overview

WEEK TWO: We Worship

Background

Jesus, the Incarnate Son of God and Savior of the world, lives today in the Church, which is the new People of God, the Body of Christ, and the Temple of the Holy Spirit. The Church's liturgy roots us in the great love that the Father has for us in his beloved Son (see Ephesians 2:4). Through the celebration of the Sacraments, we are made sharers in the Passion, Death, Resurrection, and glorious Ascension of Jesus Christ.

During Week Two, the children will explore the third and fourth units of the *Be My Disciples* curriculum, We Worship: Part One and We Worship: Part Two. Both as a large group and in their age- or grade-level learning groups, they will focus on how the Sacraments bind us together as a community of faith and how we worship as Catholics. They will explore the key faith concepts listed below, and will have the opportunity to celebrate Mass on Day 10.

KEY FAITH CONCEPTS

- **Sacraments of Christian Initiation: Baptism, Confirmation, and Eucharist**

- **Sacraments of Healing: Penance and Reconciliation, and the Anointing of the Sick**

- **Sacraments at the Service of Communion: Matrimony and Holy Orders**

- **The Church's liturgical year**

The Church Teaches ...

The *General Directory for Catechesis* (GDC) reminds us:

> Liturgical catechesis prepares for the sacraments by promoting a deeper understanding and experience of the liturgy. This explains the contents of the prayers, the meaning of the signs and gestures, educates to active participation, contemplation and silence. It must be regarded as an "eminent kind of catechesis."   *GDC* 71

Further Reading and Reflection

For more on the teachings of the Catholic Church on the celebration of the Christian mystery, see *Catechism of the Catholic Church* paragraphs 1066-1690, and *United States Catholic Catechism for Adults*, pages 165-303.

DAILY HIGHLIGHTS

Days 6-9 Each four-hour session includes warm-up and focusing activities, prayer celebrations, and age- or grade-level learning groups in which the children explore chapters from Unit 3 and Unit 4 in the *Be My Disciples* student book. The sessions include a break for fun and refreshments. Let's Wrap It Up concludes each session with presentations of activities, Disciple Power virtues, and closing prayer.

Week Two WE WORSHIP	Day 6 Give Thanks	Day 7 Live in the Spirit	Day 8 Increase Our Faith	Day 9 Light of the World	Day 10 Give Glory to God
Scripture	Psalm 118:29	Galatians 5:22–23, 25	Luke 17:5–6	Matthew 5:14,16	1 Corinthians 10:31
Faith Focus	•The Church celebrates liturgical seasons. •The Sacraments are the heart of the Church's liturgy. •Through the Church's liturgical celebrations, we give thanks to God.	•In the celebration of Confirmation, we use specific words and actions. •The Fruits of the Spirit show that we live in and follow the Spirit.	•Our participation in the sacramental life of the Church increases our faith. •Our families are families of faith.	•We are called to be the light of the world. •The Sacraments nourish us to be lights in the world.	•The Sacraments give us the grace we need to do everything for the glory of God. •We celebrate and share in the Eucharist. **Liturgical Year:** Triduum/Holy Thursday **Catholic Social Teaching:** Dignity of work and the rights of workers; option for poor and vulnerable
Discover, Part One	Learning Groups • Chapter 9	Learning Groups • Chapter 11	Learning Groups • Chapter 13	Learning Groups • Chapter 15	Activity Centers •Enriching the Lesson •Catholic Social Teaching •Liturgical Year
Discover, Part Two	Learning Groups • Chapter 10	Learning Groups • Chapter 12	Learning Groups • Chapter 14	Learning Groups • Chapter 16	Learning Groups •We Celebrate the Mass •Mass Preparation •Mass *(Families and Parish Community invited)*
Let's Wrap It Up	• Activity sharing • Disciple Power presentations	• Activity sharing • Disciple Power presentations	• Activity sharing • Disciple Power presentations	• Activity sharing • Disciple Power presentations	• Interactive Gallery • Potluck Meal

DAY 10

Activity Centers   During the first part of the session, the children will participate in activity centers (see Day 5, or pages 18-19 for an explanation).

We Celebrate the Mass   The second part of the Day 10 session includes presenting the We Celebrate the Mass activities in the student book, Mass preparation, and the celebration of Mass. Invite parents, family members, and other parishioners to this celebration. Adapt and design this day's session to best fit the needs and resources of your group.

Interactive Gallery   Invite parents, family members, and other parishioners to visit this showcase of the children's work after the celebration of Mass.

Give Thanks

"Give thanks to the Lord, who is good, whose love endures forever."

(Psalm 118:29)

Background

Around the world, Catholics are giving thanks to God every day in every moment through the Church's liturgical life—Sunday, the Lord's Day, and her liturgical seasons and celebrations.

Like an eternal spiral, the liturgical cycle invites us deeper and deeper into the mystery of Christ's life, Death, and Resurrection. These seasons of faith are the Church's gifts to us; as they return each year, they call us forward once again into the heart of the Christian story. The liturgical seasons are markers on our journey of growth and transformation. They are opportunities for us to worship and give thanks to God whose goodness and love endures forever.

In Today's Session ... In Chapters 9 and 10 of each of their grade levels, the children will learn: the Church's liturgical seasons; Sunday is the Lord's Day; we worship God through words and actions; we celebrate the Sacraments; when we pray we thank and praise God; the liturgy is the official prayer of the Church; the Creeds summarize Catholic belief; and the Sacraments make the saving work of Jesus present. They will learn about Disciple Power virtues, explore ways people of faith have lived these virtues, and be challenged to make faith choices about ways they can be disciples of Jesus.

Faith Focus

- The Church celebrates liturgical seasons.
- The Sacraments are the heart of the Church's liturgy.
- Through the Church's liturgical celebrations, we give thanks to God.

My Planning Notes DAY 6

_____
_____
_____
_____
_____
_____
_____
_____
_____
_____

Getting Started

In Advance

☐ Check in with your catechists and learning group leaders.

- Review the day's schedule.

- Explain and assign responsibilities for the Welcome, Let's Take A Break, and Let's Wrap It Up activities and prayers.

- Address any age- or grade- level specific needs your catechists may have, including materials needed.

- Remind the catechists to choose with their children one activity from the day's chapters to present to the large group during Let's Wrap It Up. Remind them to choose a creative strategy for presenting the two Disciple Power virtues to the large group (see pages 20-21), and to leave a bit of time at the end of their second session to plan the presentation.

☐ Set up the large group meeting space.

☐ Create and post a We Worship wall by taping several sheets of newsprint together on a wall or board. Write We Worship in large letters at the top of the newsprint. If possible, leave this up in your meeting space during the Summer Program, or, if necessary, carefully remove and store for the next day.

☐ Prepare the prayer environment.

☐ Gather materials for large group activities, and create a set of index cards that have the Disciple Power virtues learned in last week's sessions written on them, one virtue per card.

☐ Have leaders cut out the Disciple Power words each group will learn (from Chapters 9 and10) using colorful construction paper. You will post these during the Let's Wrap It Up segment to continue the creation of a Disciple Power collage.

☐ Ask leaders to make a set of Faith Vocabulary/Faith Words cards from the two chapters. If time permits, you can use these cards during the Let's Wrap It Up segment in today's session.

☐ Optional: Assign someone to be the photographer or videographer for the *Be My Disciples* Digital Scrapbook (see pages 18-19). Set up the digital scrapbook to be showing as the children enter the session.

Materials

☐ Bible, candle, cross, cloth for prayer space

☐ *Be My Disciples* student books

☐ Newsprint, markers, and tape

☐ CD player and *Be My Disciples* Music CD

☐ Optional: projector, screen for Digital Scrapbook

WELCOME

You and the catechists should be on hand to greet the children when they arrive. This will help them feel safe and ready to learn.

ICEBREAKER

- Invite all of the children to gather in the large meeting space.

- Play a large group icebreaker. Divide the children into mixed-age groups of four to six. Give each group one of the Disciple Power cards you made (see In Advance). Tell the children not to let any other group see the word on their cards. Give them five minutes to create a charade or pantomime skit which demonstrates the virtue on the card. They cannot use any words, just actions. The goal is for the other participants to guess what virtue is being demonstrated.

LET'S GET FOCUSED

- Invite the children to join their catechists to form the program's age- or grade- level learning groups. Have them remain in the large group meeting space.

- In their groups, have the catechists facilitate a brief discussion of the children's earliest memories of "going to church", and first memories of learning about God and about prayer. You may want to introduce the discussion in the large group by sharing from your own experience the "who, what, when, why, and where" of your own earliest memories.

- Invite volunteers from each learning group to share highlights of what they discussed.

- Ask volunteers to name aloud the seasons of the Church year. List them on newsprint as they are named (Advent, Christmas, Lent, Triduum, Easter, and Ordinary Time). Then, take a tally of the children's favorite seasons of the Church year.

- Point out the theme for the session, Give Thanks. Ask the children to name some of the things that they want to thank God for. Suggest that the liturgies we celebrate, including the Mass on Sunday, the Sacraments, and all of the Church's experiences of prayer and worship are opportunities the Church gives us to thank God for his goodness and love.

Bless Us, Lord

• Ask the children to bow their heads, close their eyes for a brief moment, and remember that God is present with them in this time and place.

• Pray together the Sign of the Cross.

 Begin today's opening prayer with the song, "Here I Am Lord" from the *Be My Disciples* Music Program, Grade 3 or Grade 5 CD.

• Invite a child to read aloud Psalm 118:29 from the Bible.

• Pose the question: For what are you thankful today?

• End with the prayer, followed by the Sign of the Cross.

Holy and gracious God, your blessings are more than we could ever count.

We thank and praise you for your gifts.

We thank and praise you for your loving presence with us today.

Amen.

DISCOVER, Part One

INTRODUCE

• Briefly describe the overall schedule for the day. Share any housekeeping information.

• Write the word *worship* in the middle of a large sheet of newsprint. Create a mind map with the children. Have them call out words and phrases that come to mind when they see the word *worship,* and write these words and phrases on the newsprint.

• Facilitate a large group brainstorming in response to this question: How do Catholics worship? At this point, do not write anything on the *We Worship* wall.

• Write these two statements on the *We Worship* wall:

   –The Church celebrates liturgical seasons.

   –The Sacraments are at the heart of the Church's liturgy.

• Suggest to the children that these are two truths that we believe and will learn more about.

TEACH, REINFORCE, CONNECT

• Tell the children that they are now going to meet in their age- or grade- level groups to discover more about what we believe as Catholics.

• Invite the catechists to gather their children, and proceed to their assigned rooms.

• Allow groups to meet for approximately one hour.

AT A GLANCE PART ONE

Each age- or grade- level group will process through Chapter 9 in the student books using the Explore, Discover, and Decide methodology of the *Be My Disciples* curriculum. Here is an overview of the faith concepts and Disciple Power virtue for each grade. Groups will share about their Disciple Power virtues in the large group Let's Wrap It Up activity.

GRADE 1 Chapter 9: The Church Celebrates Jesus
The Church has special times and seasons of the year; Sunday is the Lord's Day.
Disciple Power: prudence

GRADE 2 Chapter 9: We Celebrate God's Love
We worship God using words and actions; the Holy Spirit helps us celebrate the Sacraments and worship God.
Disciple Power: piety

GRADE 3 Chapter 9: A People of Prayer
We pray for ourselves and others; we bless God who gives us all blessings; we thank and praise God.
Disciple Power: patience

GRADE 4 Chapter 9: People of Prayer
The Church is a people of prayer; the liturgy is the Church's official prayer; the creeds are short summaries of the faith of the Church.
Disciple Power: wonder and awe

GRADE 5 Chapter 9: Celebrating the Liturgy
The liturgy is the Church's work of worshiping God; the Sacraments make up the saving work of Jesus Christ; the liturgical year is the Church's cycle of worship.
Disciple Power: perseverance

GRADE 6 Chapter 9: Celebrating the Liturgy
Liturgy is the Church's work of worshiping God; the Seven Sacraments are at the center of the Church's liturgy; the Church celebrates throughout the year.
Disciple Power: diligence

LET'S TAKE A BREAK!

When the age- or grade- level groups have completed their work with the first chapter for the day, invite them to join together with all of the children in the program for refreshments and play time. (Note: Some groups may finish before others. To avoid distractions for the groups still meeting, if possible, set up the break time activities away from the meeting spaces.)

DISCOVER, Part Two

INTRODUCE

- Invite all of the children to gather in the large group meeting space with their learning groups.

- Direct their attention to the We Worship wall. Going from group to group, ask the participants to name things they learned in their first session about how and why Catholics worship.

- Write or have volunteers write responses on the wall.

TEACH, REINFORCE, CONNECT

- Tell the children that they are now going to meet in their age- or grade- level groups to discover more about what we believe as Catholics.

- Invite the catechists to gather their children, and proceed to their assigned rooms.

- Allow groups to meet for approximately 1 hour, 15 minutes.

LET'S WRAP IT UP!

REINFORCE

- Invite all of the children to gather, with their catechists, in the main meeting space.
- Direct everyone's attention once again to the We Worship wall. Going from group to group, ask the participants to name things they learned in their second session about Catholic worship.
- Write or have volunteers write responses on the newsprint.
- Summarize the learning for the large group.
- Collect the extra set of Faith Vocabulary/ Faith Words cards that each group has made.

WE REMEMBER

- Invite each group to present the one activity they have chosen to share from their chapters.
- Have each group present its Disciple Power virtues. Continue making the Disciple Power collage by adding today's virtues to it.
- If time permits, play Name that Faith Word (see page 34).

WE PRAY

- Choose the prayer from either Chapter 9 or Chapter 10 in the grade-level student books to pray together as a large group. Or use the following prayer ritual.
- Have everyone gather in the prayer space.

AT A GLANCE PART TWO

Each age- or grade- level group will process through Chapter 10 in the student books. Here is an overview of the faith concepts and Disciple Power virtue for each grade.

GRADE 1 Chapter 10: Signs of God's Love
In Baptism, God shares his love and life with us; we receive the gift of the Holy Spirit; in Confirmation we are sealed with the gift of the Holy Spirit to help us live out our Baptism.
Disciple Power: hospitality

GRADE 2 Chapter 10: Our Church Welcomes Us
Baptism is the first Sacrament we receive; Baptism joins us to Christ and each other; the words and actions of Baptism show that we share in God's life.
Disciple Power: faith

GRADE 3 Chapter 10: The Church Year
The liturgy is the Church's public worship; the liturgical year includes Advent, Christmas, Lent, Easter, and Ordinary Time.
Disciple Power: love

GRADE 4 Chapter 10: Celebrating God's Love
The liturgy is the Church's work of worshiping God; in the liturgy we are made sharers in the Paschal Mystery; the Church shares and celebrates God's plan of Salvation.
Disciple Power: truthfulness

GRADE 5 Chapter 10: Joined to Christ
Baptism, Confirmation, and Eucharist are the three Sacraments of Christian Initiation; Baptism joins us to Christ; in Baptism Original Sin and all.
Disciple Power: generosity

GRADE 6 Chapter 10: Baptism
Baptism is the first Sacrament; through Baptism we receive the gift of the Holy Spirit; a person becomes fully initiated into the Church through the Sacraments of Christian Initiation.
Disciple Power: modesty

We Pray

- Begin prayer by singing "Our God is Here" from the *Be My Disciples* Music Program, Grade 3 or Grade 5 CD.
- Light a candle and pray together the Sign of the Cross.
- Pray Psalm 118 in its entirety. (Suggestion: Invite seven children, in advance, to each proclaim one of the seven stanzas of the psalm.)

TO TAKE HOME

Have the children take home the Chapter Review and With My Family page from Chapters 9 and 10 to share with their families.

Live in the Spirit

"… [T]he fruit of the Spirit is love, joy, peace, patience, kindness, generosity, faithfulness, gentleness, self-control. … If we live in the Spirit, let us also follow the Spirit".

(Galatians 5:22-23, 25)

Background

Baptism, the first Sacrament we receive, is closely related to Confirmation. Baptism is the entry door into life in the Church and is one of the three Sacraments of Christian Initiation. Through Baptism we are joined to Christ and become part of the Body of Christ, the Church. Confirmation completes the grace of Baptism by a special outpouring of the Gifts of the Holy Spirit. The Holy Spirit is always with us as our companion and guide.

With the help of the Holy Spirit, Christians are called to transform the most mundane activities of daily life into the riches of the Kingdom of God. It may be when we are rushing to the grocery store that we are asked to feed someone else. It may be when we want to spend some time alone that we become aware of the need of another person. Jesus asks us to love as he loves, and to offer the gifts of love, forgiveness, gratitude, tenderness, and compassion to others. The sacramental life of our Church strengthens us to do so.

In Today's Session … In Chapters 11 and 12 of each of the grade levels, the children will learn: the Gospel is the Good News of Jesus; the Holy Spirit gives us spiritual gifts; Baptism joins us to Christ; Confirmation strengthens our Baptism; the Sacraments of Christian Initiation join us to Christ and make us full members of the Church; and the Gifts of the Holy Spirit empower us to continue the mission of Christ. They will also learn: Christian families are signs of Jesus' love in the world; the effects of the Sacraments of Penance and Reconciliation and the Anointing of the Sick; the vocation of the baptized; the Eucharist is the center of the Christian life; and the Mass recalls and makes present the one sacrifice of Christ. They will learn about Disciple Power virtues, explore ways people of faith have lived those virtues, and be challenged to make faith choices about ways they can be disciples of Jesus.

Faith Focus

• In the celebration of Confirmation, we use specific words and actions.

• The Fruits of the Holy Spirit show that we live in the Spirit.

My Planning Notes
DAY 7

_____
_____
_____
_____
_____
_____

Getting Started

In Advance

❑ Check in with your catechists and learning group leaders.

- Review the day's schedule.

- Explain and assign responsibilities for the Welcome, Let's Take A Break, and Let's Wrap It Up activities and prayers.

- Address any age- or grade- level specific needs your catechists may have, including materials needed for their student chapter activities.

- Remind the catechists to choose with their children one activity to present to the large group during Let's Wrap It Up. Remind them to choose a creative strategy for presenting the two Disciple Power virtues to the large group (see pages 20-21), and to leave a bit of time at the end of their second session to plan the presentation.

❑ Set up the large group meeting space.

❑ Post the We Worship wall in the large group gathering space.

❑ Prepare the prayer environment.

❑ Gather materials for large group activities.

- For the Warm Up, you will need index cards and pens or pencils.

- Make Fruits of the Spirit cards by writing one of the following on each card: love, joy, peace, patience, kindness, generosity, faithfulness, gentleness, and self-control.

❑ Have leaders cut out the Disciple Power words each group will learn (from Chapters 11 and 12) using colorful construction paper. You will post these during the Let's Wrap It Up segment to continue the creation of a Disciple Power collage.

❑ Ask leaders to make a set of Faith Vocabulary/ Faith Words cards from the two chapters. You will use these cards during Day 10, and, if time permits, during the Let's Wrap It Up segment in today's session.

❑ Optional: Assign someone to be the photographer or videographer for the *Be My Disciples* Digital Scrapbook (see pages 18-19). Set up the digital scrapbook to be showing as the children enter the session.

WELCOME

You and the catechists should be on hand to greet the children when they arrive. This will help them feel safe and ready to learn.

ICEBREAKER

• Invite all of the children to gather in the large meeting space.

• Play an icebreaker called Whodunit? Select a group of ten or more volunteers. Include a mix of ages and adult leaders. Give each volunteer an index card and pen. Have them write something interesting they have done, or that has happened to them, on the card. (For example, I went skydiving. I've eaten bugs. I got straight A's. I won a tennis tournament.) Collect the cards and shuffle them. Randomly draw the cards, one by one, and call out to the large group what is written on the card. The object is to guess "Whodunit?" from the group of volunteers. (You can also divide the large group into smaller groups to play the game. This way, everyone has a chance to fill out a whodunit card.)

LET'S GET FOCUSED

• Find volunteers to form nine pairs of partners. Distribute one of the nine Fruits of the Spirit cards to each of the pairs. The pair's task is to describe the word on the card to the large group without ever actually saying the word. Encourage the partners to describe the word by giving an example of someone who actually "lives" the word. Have the children see if they can guess the correct words.

• Tell the children that the words they have seen described are the Fruits of the Holy Spirit. Saint Paul tells us that, if we live in the Spirit, we follow the Spirit. These "Fruits" are evidence.

• Ask the children to gather in the prayer space. As they gather, tape the Fruits of the Holy Spirit cards to the We Worship wall.

- Ask the children to bow their heads, close their eyes for a brief moment, and remember that God is present with them in this time and place.

- Pray together the Sign of the Cross.

- Invite a child to read aloud Galatians 5:22-23, 25 from the Bible.

- Pose the question: Which Fruit of the Spirit can others see in your words and actions? How? Invite the children to share with a partner.

- End with the prayer, followed by the Sign of the Cross.

Bless Us, Lord

God our Father and Creator, through the waters of Baptism we are joined to Christ, your Son. Send the Holy Spirit to be with us and bless us as we learn to live as your children. Amen.

 End today's prayer by singing "We are Called" from the *Be My Disciples* Music Program, Grade 4 or Grade 6 CD.

DISCOVER, Part One

INTRODUCE

- Briefly describe the overall schedule for program, and more specifically for the day. Share any housekeeping information.

- Point out the We Worship wall and the Fruits of the Holy Spirit cards. Tell the children that today they will learn more about how the Church worships, and how the Holy Spirit guides and strengthens us to be Jesus' disciples.

AT A GLANCE PART ONE

Each age- or grade- level group will process through Chapter 11 in the student books using the Explore, Discover, and Decide methodology of the Be My Disciples curriculum. Here is an overview of the faith concepts and Disciple Power virtue for each grade. Groups will share about their Disciple Power virtues in the large group Let's Wrap It Up activity.

GRADE 1 Chapter 11: We Follow Jesus
The Gospel is the Good News that Jesus told us about God's love; we tell everyone about the Good News.
Disciple Power: goodness

GRADE 2 Chapter 11: We Celebrate the Holy Spirit
In the Sacrament of Confirmation, the Holy Spirit strengthens us to live our Baptism; the Holy Spirit gives us spiritual gifts to help us love and serve God and one another.
Disciple Power: knowledge

GRADE 3 Chapter 11: Celebrating God's Love
The Sacraments of Christian Initiation lay the foundation for our lives as disciples of Jesus; Baptism joins us to Christ and the Church; Confirmation strengthens our Baptism.
Disciple Power: fortitude

GRADE 4 Chapter 11: Sharing in Christ's Life and Work
Christ gave the Church the Seven Sacraments; by receiving the Sacraments of Christian Initiation, we are fully joined to Christ and become full members of the Church.
Disciple Power: knowledge

GRADE 5 Chapter 11: We Celebrate the Holy Spirit
Christ means "anointed one"; in Confirmation we are sealed with the gift of the Holy Spirit; with the Gifts of the Holy Spirit we are empowered to continue the mission of Christ.
Disciple Power: understanding

GRADE 6 Grade 6 Chapter 11: Confirmation
The Sacrament of Confirmation perfects the grace of Baptism; the Rite of Confirmation includes the laying on of hands and anointing with oil by the bishop; Confirmation strengthens us to be living witnesses to Christ.
Disciple Power: fortitude

TEACH, REINFORCE, CONNECT

- Tell the children that they are now going to meet in their age- or grade- level groups to discover more about Catholic prayer and worship.

- Invite the catechists to gather their children, and proceed to their classrooms or meeting rooms.

- Allow groups to meet for approximately one hour.

LET'S TAKE A BREAK!

When the age- or grade- level groups have completed their work with the first chapter for the day, invite them to join together with all of the children in the program for refreshments and play time. (Note: Some groups may finish before others. To avoid distractions for the groups still meeting, if possible, set up the Break Time activities away from the meeting spaces.)

DISCOVER, Part Two

INTRODUCE

- Invite all of the children to gather in the large group meeting space with their learning groups.

- Direct their attention to the We Worship wall. Going from group to group, ask the participants to name things they learned in their first session about how and why Catholics worship.

- Write or have volunteers write responses on the newsprint.

TEACH, REINFORCE, CONNECT

- Tell the children that they are now going to meet in their age- or grade- level groups to discover more about how Catholics worship.

- Invite the catechists to proceed with their children to their classrooms or meeting rooms.

- Allow groups to meet for approximately 1 hour, 15 minutes.

AT A GLANCE PART TWO

Each age or grade- level group will process through Chapter 12 in the student books. Here is an overview of the faith concepts and Disciple Power virtue for each grade.

GRADE 1 Chapter 12: The Catholic Family
Christian families are signs of God's love in the world; members of a family share their love for God and one another; our family helps us live our faith.
Disciple Power: fidelity

GRADE 2 Chapter 12: We Celebrate Forgiveness
Sin is choosing to do or say something against God; in the Sacrament of Penance and Reconciliation, we ask for and receive forgiveness for our sins.
Disciple Power: forgiveness

GRADE 3 Chapter 12: God's Healing Love
In the Sacrament of Penance and Reconciliation, God forgives our sins; in the Sacrament of the Anointing of the Sick, our faith and trust in God are made stronger.
Disciple Power: kindness

GRADE 4 Chapter 12: Responding to God's Call
God calls all the baptized to do the work of the Church; every person who is baptized has a vocation to know, love, and serve God.
Disciple Power: joy

GRADE 5 Chapter 12: One Bread, One Cup
Jesus gave us the Eucharist; the celebration of the Sacrament of the Eucharist renews and makes present the one sacrifice of Christ; the Eucharist is the center of Christian life.
Disciple Power: charity

GRADE 6 Chapter 12: The Eucharist
Events in the Old Testament prefigure the mystery of the Eucharist; the Mass recalls and makes present the one sacrifice of Christ; the Eucharist is the memorial of the Paschal Mystery.
Disciple Power: faithfulness

LET'S WRAP IT UP!

REINFORCE

- Invite all of the children to gather, with their catechists, in the main meeting space.

- Direct everyone's attention once again to the We Worship wall. Going from group to group, ask the participants to name things they learned in their second session about Catholic prayer and worship.

- Write or have volunteers write responses on the newsprint.

- Summarize the learning for the large group.

- Collect the extra set of Faith Vocabulary/Faith Words cards that each group has made.

WE REMEMBER

- Invite each group to present the one activity they have chosen to share from their chapters.

- Have each group present its Disciple Power virtues. Continue making the Disciple Power collage by adding today's virtues to it.

- If time permits, play Name that Faith Word (see page 34).

WE PRAY

- Choose the prayer from one of the student books, Chapter 11 or 12, to pray together as a large group. Or, use the following prayer.

We Pray

Have the children form a circle for prayer. Begin with the Sign of the Cross.

Leader: Together let us ask God for the presence of his Spirit in our lives, so that we may live as disciples of Jesus, God's Son.

Leader: For a spirit of love, we pray-
All: Lord, hear our prayer.

Leader: For a spirit of joy, we pray-
All: Lord, hear our prayer.

Leader: For a spirit of peace, we pray-
All: Lord, hear our prayer.

Leader: For a spirit of patience, we pray-
All: Lord, hear our prayer.

Leader: For a spirit of kindness, we pray-
All: Lord, hear our prayer.

Leader: For a spirit of generosity, we pray-
All: Lord, hear our prayer.

Leader: For a spirit of faithfulness, we pray-
All: Lord, hear our prayer.

Leader: For a spirit of gentleness we pray-
All: Lord, hear our prayer.

Leader: For a spirit of self-control, we pray-
All: Lord, hear our prayer.

End today's prayer with "We Are Called" from the *Be My Disciples* Music Program, Grade 2, Grade 4, or Grade 6 CD.

TO TAKE HOME

Remind the catechists and group leaders to have the children take home the Chapter Review and With My Family page from Chapters 11 and 12 to share with their families.

Increase Our Faith

"And the apostles said to the Lord, "Increase our faith." The Lord replied, "If you have faith the size of a mustard seed, you would say to [this] mulberry tree, 'Be uprooted and planted in the sea,' and it would obey you."

(Luke 17:5-6)

Background

Sometimes belief is a struggle, but the gift of faith brings certainty. The challenge for Christians is to respond to the message of Jesus – to live out by word and example his command to love one another. Knowing, believing, and living lives of virtue form the identity of people of faith.

Faith, hope, and love can flourish in our parish communities and in our families. These are environments in which our faith can increase. Everything the children are learning in *Be My Disciples* is intended to help them grow in faith. As they learn, grow, share, and pray together, they can hear Jesus' gentle response to the disciples' plea, "Increase our faith."

In Today's Session ... In Chapters 13 and 14 of each of their age- or grade- levels the children will explore and learn faith concepts including: prayer; the Mass; the parables of Jesus; the Bible; Jesus calls us to forgive and to ask for forgiveness; the Sacrament of Penance and Reconciliation; the effects of sin; the Liturgy of the Word; the Liturgy of the Eucharist; the Church continues Jesus' work of healing and forgiveness; and the effects of the Anointing of the Sick. They will learn about Disciple Power virtues, explore ways people of faith have lived those virtues, and be challenged to make faith choices about ways they can be disciples of Jesus.

Faith Focus

- Our participation in the sacramental life of the Church increases our faith.

- Our families are families of faith.

My Planning Notes
DAY 8
_____
_____
_____
_____
_____
_____
_____
_____
_____

Getting Started

In Advance

❑ Check in with your catechists and learning group leaders.

- Review the day's schedule.

- Explain and assign responsibilities as needed for the Welcome, Let's Take A Break, and Let's Wrap It Up activities and prayers.

- Address any age- or grade- level specific needs your catechists may have, including materials needed.

- Remind the catechists to choose with their children one activity from the day's chapters to present to the large group during Let's Wrap It Up. Remind them to choose a creative strategy for presenting the two Disciple Power virtues to the large group (see pages 20-21), and to leave a bit of time at the end of their second session to plan the presentation.

❑ Set up the large group meeting space. Post the We Worship wall..

❑ Prepare the prayer environment.

❑ Gather materials for large group activities.

- Make Telephone Charade clues (see Icebreaker on page 78).

- Write "Faith can move mountains" scrambled on a sheet of newsprint. For example, "iahtf nca emvo tmsnoiuan."

❑ Have leaders cut out the Disciple Power words each group will learn (from Chapters 13 and 14) using colorful construction paper. You will post these during the Let's Wrap It Up segment to continue the creation of a Disciple Power collage.

❑ Ask leaders to make a set of Faith Vocabulary/Faith Words cards from the two chapters. You will use these cards during Day 10, and, if time permits, during the Let's Wrap It Up segment in today's session.

❑ Optional: Assign someone to be the photographer or videographer for the *Be My Disciples* Digital Scrapbook (see pages 18-19). Set up the digital scrapbook to be showing as the children enter the session.

Materials

❑ Bible, candle, cross, cloth for prayer space

❑ *Be My Disciples* student books

❑ Newsprint, markers, and tape

❑ CD player and *Be My Disciples* Music CD

❑ Optional: projector, screen for Digital Scrapbook

WELCOME

You and the catechists should be on hand to greet the children when they arrive. This will help them feel safe and ready to learn.

ICEBREAKER

- Invite all of the children to gather in the large meeting space.

- Play a large group icebreaker such as Telephone Charades. To prepare for the game, write (in large letters) humorous actions to be acted out, each on a sheet of paper. Some examples are: a first date, a cat bathing itself, going skydiving, a bird sitting on its nest, fishing and catching a huge fish. To play, ask five or six volunteers to come to the front of the room and to line up in a row, facing the left side of the room. Ask the first person to turn around to see the first clue to be acted out. Reveal the clue to the person, and display the clue to the audience as well. The first person turns around and taps the next person in line on the shoulder. He or she then acts out the clue using classic charades rules (no talking or noises permitted). The second person then taps the third person and acts out his or her understanding of what was acted out. This process continues until it reaches the last person in line, who must guess what the action is. This game is funny because the acting tends to warp and get distorted based upon each person's interpretation of what is going on.

LET'S GET FOCUSED

- Tell the participants that you are going to post a newsprint that has a scrambled sentence on it. The children can work together in pairs or small groups to unscramble the sentence. Post the newsprint ("faith can move mountains" scrambled), and let the children unscramble it.

- Invite volunteers to tell what the sentence means. Listen to responses, and circle the word *faith* in the sentence. Suggest that faith is not a thing, it is an action. Ask the group to reflect on the question, "What does it mean to live your faith?", as they gather in the prayer space for the opening prayer.

Bless Us, Lord

- Ask the children to bow their heads, close their eyes for a brief moment, and remember that God is present with them in this time and place.

   Sing or play, "Christ be Our Light" from the *Be My Disciples* Music Program, Grade 2 CD.

- Light a candle and lead the participants in praying the Sign of the Cross.
- Invite a volunteer to read aloud Luke 17: 5-6 from the Bible.
- Pose the question: What are the qualities of a person who lives his or her faith? Invite the children to share with a partner. Canvas the room to discover some of the qualities the children discussed.
- End with the prayer, followed by the Sign of the Cross.

Gracious God,

we are grateful

for your presence

in our lives.

Faith in you has

the power to

change lives.

Help us be

people of faith.

Amen.

DISCOVER, Part One

INTRODUCE

- Briefly describe the overall schedule for the day. Share any housekeeping information.
- Review the We Worship wall, and tell the children they will continue their learning and discovery of how we worship.

AT A GLANCE PART ONE

Each age- or grade- level group will process through Chapter 13 in the student books using the Explore, Discover, and Decide methodology of the *Be My Disciples* curriculum. Here is an overview of the faith concepts and Disciple Power virtue for each grade. Groups will share a creative presentation of their Disciple Power virtues in the Let's Wrap It Up activity.

GRADE 1 Chapter 13: We Pray
Prayer is listening and talking to God; when we pray we grow in our love for God; God always listens to our prayers.
Disciple Power: patience

GRADE 2 Chapter 13: We Gather for Mass
The Mass is the most important celebration of the Church; everyone at Mass has a part to play; the Introductory Rites gather us and prepare us to worship God.
Disciple Power: love

GRADE 3 Chapter 13: The Word of God
A parable is a story used to teach people; Catholics have the obligation to take part in the Mass on Sunday; the Liturgy of the Word is the first main part of the liturgy.
Disciple Power: understanding

GRADE 4 Chapter 13: Jesus Feeds Us
During the Exodus, God fed the Israelites with manna, Jesus fed five thousand people with five loaves of bread and two fish; the Bible invites us to trust in God's loving care for us.
Disciple Power: kindness

GRADE 5 Chapter 13: Jesus Heals the Sinner
Jesus calls his disciples to forgive and to ask for forgiveness; the Sacrament of Penance and Reconciliation continues Jesus' ministry of healing; in this Sacrament we are forgiven the sins we commit after we are baptized.
Disciple Power: mercy

GRADE 6 Grade 6
Chapter 13: Penance and Reconciliation
The Rite of Penance has a movement of conversion that includes repentance, confession, and absolution; in Penance and Reconciliation we receive God's forgiveness for sins committed after Baptism.
Disciple Power: self-control

TEACH, REINFORCE, CONNECT

- Tell the children that they are now going to meet again in their age- or grade-level groups to discover more about Catholics and worship.

- Invite the catechists to proceed with their children to their classrooms or meeting rooms.

- Allow groups to meet for approximately one hour.

LET'S TAKE A BREAK!

When the age- or grade- level groups have completed their work with the first chapter for the day, invite them to join together with all of the children in the program for refreshments and play time. (Note: Some groups may finish before others. To avoid distractions for the groups still meeting, if possible, set up the Let's Take a Break activities away from the meeting spaces.)

DISCOVER, Part Two

INTRODUCE

- Invite all of the children to gather in the large group meeting space with their learning groups.

- Direct their attention to the We Worship wall. Going from group to group, ask the participants to name things they learned in the day's first session about how Catholics worship.

- Write or have volunteers write responses on the newsprint

TEACH, REINFORCE, CONNECT

- Tell the children that they are now going to meet again in their age- or grade- level groups to discover more about how we worship as Catholics.

- Invite the catechists to proceed with their children to their classrooms or meeting rooms.

- Allow groups to meet for approximately 1 hour, 15 minutes.

AT A GLANCE PART TWO

Each age- or grade- level group will process through Chapter 14 in the student books. Here is an overview of the faith concepts and Disciple Power virtue for each grade.

GRADE 1 Chapter 14: We are Peacemakers
Sin hurts our relationship with God and others; when we say we are sorry we show that we love God and others.
Disciple Power: peace

GRADE 2 Chapter 14: We Listen to God's Word
The Liturgy of the Word is the first main part of the Mass; the Gospel is the main part of the Liturgy of the Word; at Mass we listen and respond to the Word of God.
Disciple Power: compassion

GRADE 3 Chapter 14: The Bread of Life
At the Eucharist we celebrate what Jesus did at the Last Supper; at Eucharist bread and wine become the Body and Blood of Christ; the Eucharist is the Blessed Sacrament.
Disciple Power: goodness

GRADE 4 Chapter 14: Jesus Forgives
Jesus continues his work of healing and forgiveness through the Church; in the acrament of Penance and Reconciliation we receive forgiveness for sins and the grace to say no to sin in the future.
Disciple Power: forgiveness

GRADE 5 Chapter 14: Jesus Heals the Sick
Through the Anointing of the Sick, those who are seriously ill, weakened because of old age, or dying are joined to the suffering of Christ and receive strength and courage.
Disciple Power: kindness

GRADE 6 Chapter 14: Anointing of the Sick
The Church continues Jesus' ministry of healing in the Sacraments of Healing; the Rite of Anointing consists of the prayer of faith, laying on of hands, and the anointing with oil.
Disciple Power: gentleness

LET'S WRAP IT UP!

REINFORCE

- Invite all of the children to gather, with their catechists, in the main meeting space.
- Direct everyone's attention once again to the We Worship wall. Going from group to group, ask the participants to name things they learned in their second session about how Catholics worship.
- Write or have volunteers write responses on the newsprint.
- Summarize the learning for the large group.
- Collect the extra set of Faith Vocabulary/Faith Words cards from each group.

WE REMEMBER

- Have the learning groups present the one activity they have chosen to share from their chapters.
- Have each group present its Disciple Power virtues. Continue making the Disciple Power collage by adding today's virtues to it.
- If time permits, play Name that Faith Word (see page 34).

WE PRAY

- Choose the prayer from one of the grade level books from either Chapter 13 or Chapter 14 to pray together as a large group. Or use the following prayer ritual.
- The psalms are songs of faith that were known and sung by Jesus and are part of the Church's liturgical heritage. They celebrate the many moods of faith. Lead the participants in a quiet meditation on the psalms for today's closing prayer.

We Pray

- Ask the children to find a comfortable place and position to pray.

- Use each of these psalm verses as a meditation starter or read one of the psalms in its entirety.

Whenever I lay down and slept, the LORD preserved me to rise again (Psalm 3:6).

Even when I walk through a dark valley, I fear no harm for you are at my side; . . . (Psalm 23:4).

In you, LORD I take refuge. Into your hands I commend my spirit; you will redeem me, LORD, faithful God (Psalm 31:2, 6).

Use "A Faith-filled Heart" instrumental from the *Be My Disciples Music* Program, Grade 1, Grade 3, or Grade 5 CD as background music during prayer, allowing time for quiet meditation.

TO TAKE HOME

Remind the catechists and group leaders to have the children take home the Chapter Review and With My Family page from Chapters 13 and 14 to share with their families.

Light of the World

"You are the light of the world. . . . [Y]our light must shine before others, that they may see your good deeds and glorify your heavenly Father."

(Matthew 5:14, 16)

Background

Followers of Jesus hear his voice, listen to his call, and follow him. For them, the voice of Jesus is heard over all the other noises, voices, and sounds that seem to fill every waking moment. As the children have been learning, Jesus is heard especially clearly through the Sacraments, in which believers encounter the Risen Lord.

In the Gospel of John, the image of light (found in John 1:3-4) is juxtaposed with that of darkness. Jesus is the light who will overcome all darkness. Jesus brings light to the darkness of confusion and sin. The grace-filled moments we experience in the Sacraments provide the inspiration to become light of the world to others.

In Today's Session ... In Chapters 15 and 16 of each of their grade levels the children will explore faith concepts including: what we do at Mass; the Eucharist is the Body and Blood of Jesus; the vocation we receive at Baptism; the effects of the Sacrament of Matrimony; Holy Orders; every Christian is joined to Christ in Baptism; Jesus showed people that God cares for them; the concluding procession at Mass; the roles of bishops and priests; the effects of the Sacraments at the Service of Communion; the ministry of married couples; and the purpose of marriage.. They will learn about Disciple Power virtues, explore ways people of faith have lived those virtues, and be challenged to make faith choices about ways they can be disciples of Jesus.

Faith Focus

- We are called to be the light of the world.
- The Sacraments nourish us to be lights in the world.

My Planning Notes
DAY 9

_____
_____
_____
_____
_____
_____
_____
_____
_____
_____

Getting Started

In Advance

❏ Check in with your catechists and learning group leaders.

- Review the day's schedule.

- Explain and assign responsibilities as needed for the Welcome, Let's Take A Break, and Let's Wrap It Up activities and prayers.

- Address any age- or grade- level specific needs your catechists may have, including materials needed.

- Remind the catechists to choose with their children one activity from the day's chapters to present to the large group during Let's Wrap It Up. Remind them to choose a creative strategy for presenting the two Disciple Power virtues to the large group (see pages 20-21), and to leave a bit of time at the end of their second session to plan the presentation.

❏ Set up the large group meeting space.

❏ Post the We Worship wall.

❏ Prepare the prayer environment.

❏ Gather materials for large group activities.

- paper, pens or pencils

❏ Create a slideshow of images that depict light.

❏ Have leaders cut out the Disciple Power words each group will learn (from Chapters 15 and 16) using colorful construction paper. You will post these during the Let's Wrap It Up segment to continue the creation of a Disciple Power collage.

❏ Ask leaders to make a set of Faith Vocabulary/ Faith Words cards from the two chapters. You will use these cards during Day 10, and, if time permits, during the Let's Wrap It Up segment in today's session.

❏ Optional: Assign someone to be the photographer or videographer for the *Be My Disciples* Digital Scrapbook (see pages 18-19). Set up the digital scrapbook to be showing as the children enter the session.

Materials

❏ Bible, candle, cross, cloth for prayer space

❏ *Be My Disciples* student books

❏ Newsprint, markers, and tape

❏ Paper, pens or pencils

❏ CD player and *Be My Disciples* Music CD

❏ Projector, screen for slideshow

❏ Optional: projector, screen for Digital Scrapbook

WELCOME

You and the catechists should be on hand to greet the children when they arrive. This will help them feel safe and ready to learn.

ICEBREAKER

- As the children arrive for the day's session, invite them to gather in small groups to brainstorm a list of all of the sources of light they can think of. Distribute paper and pens, and ask each group to record its responses.

- Have volunteers read their lists to the large group.

LET'S GET FOCUSED

- Dim the lights and project the slideshow images (see In Advance, page 83) on a wall or screen at the front of the room.

- Tell the group that Jesus once told his disciples, "You are the salt of the earth." He also told them, "You are the light of the world."

- Ask: What do you think it means to be the light of the world? Listen to and summarize the responses.

Bless Us, Lord

- Ask the children to bow their heads, close their eyes for a brief moment, and remember that God is present with them in this time and place.

- Light a candle at the prayer table.

 Play "Christ Be Our Light" from the *Be My Disciples* Music Program, Grade 2 CD.

- Pray together the Sign of the Cross.

- Invite a volunteer to read aloud Matthew 5:14-16 from the Bible.

- Pose this question: Why does Jesus ask his disciples to be the light of the world? Give the children a moment to reflect and then invite them to share with partners.

- End with the prayer, followed by the Sign of the Cross.

God of all goodness, your Son Jesus shows us how we can best love you and others. He shows us how we can be light in the world by living as his disciples. Teach us today what it means to be your light. Amen.

DISCOVER, Part One

INTRODUCE

- Briefly describe the overall schedule for the day. Share any housekeeping information.

- Point out the We Worship wall. Have the catechists or learning group leaders name one or two things that their groups will discover or learn more about today.

TEACH, REINFORCE, CONNECT

- Tell the children that they are now going to meet in their age- or grade- level groups to discover more about what we believe as Catholics.

- Invite the catechists to gather their children, and proceed to their classrooms or meeting rooms.

- Allow groups to meet for approximately one hour.

AT A GLANCE PART ONE

Each age- or grade- level group will process through Chapter 15 in the student books using the Explore, Discover, and Decide methodology of the *Be My Disciples* curriculum. Here is an overview of the faith concepts and Disciple Power virtue for each grade. Groups will share a creative presentation of their Disciple Power virtues in the Let's Wrap It Up activity.

GRADE 1 Chapter 15: We Go to Mass
At Mass, we worship God; we listen to readings from the Bible; we celebrate and share in the Eucharist.
Disciple Power: perseverance

GRADE 2 Chapter 15: We Give Thanks
Jesus gave the Church the Sacrament of Eucharist at the Last Supper; at Eucharist the bread and wine become the Body and Blood of Jesus; we receive the Body and Blood of Jesus in Holy Communion.
Disciple Power: thankfulness

GRADE 3 Chapter 15: The Sacrament of Matrimony
Jesus performed a miracle at Cana to show God's power at work in the world; at Baptism we receive the vocation to share in Jesus' life and work; in Matrimony a baptized man and woman become a sign of God's love in the world.
Disciple Power: chastity

GRADE 4 Chapter 15: Jesus Heals the Sick
The Bible has many stories that describe how people deal with their sickness and suffering; we are to reach out to Jesus in faith and trust when we are sick or suffering.
Disciple Power: compassion

GRADE 5 Chapter 15: The Sacrament of Holy Orders
All of the baptized are called to continue the work of Christ; Holy Orders consecrates some men to serve the whole Church; it is one of the Sacraments at the Service of Communion.
Disciple Power: faith

GRADE 6 Chapter 15: Holy Orders
Every Christian is joined to Christ in Baptism and is called to live a life of generous service to God and others as Jesus did; Holy Orders consecrates a baptized man to serve the whole Church as a bishop, priest, or deacon.
Disciple Power: patience

LET'S TAKE A BREAK!

When the age- or grade- level groups have completed their work with the first chapter for the day, invite them to join together with all of the children in the program for refreshments and play time. (Note: Some groups may finish before others. To avoid distractions for the groups still meeting, if possible, set up the Break Time activities away from the meeting spaces.)

DISCOVER, Part Two

INTRODUCE

- Invite all of the children to gather in the large group meeting space with their learning groups.
- Direct their attention to the We Worship wall. Going from group to group, ask the participants to name things they learned in the day's first session.
- Write or have volunteers write responses on the newsprint.

TEACH, REINFORCE, CONNECT

- Tell the children that they are now going to meet again in their age- or grade- level groups to discover more about our prayer and worship as Catholics.
- Invite the catechists to proceed with their children to their classrooms or meeting rooms.
- Allow groups to meet for approximately 1 hour, 15 minutes.

LET'S WRAP IT UP!

REINFORCE

- Invite all of the children to gather, with their catechists, in the main meeting space.
- Direct everyone's attention once again to the We Worship wall. Going from group to group, ask the participants to name things they learned in their second session about how Catholics worship.
- Write or have volunteers write responses on the newsprint.
- Summarize the learning for the large group.
- Collect the extra set of Faith Vocabulary/Faith Words cards that each group has made. Save these for Day 10.

AT A GLANCE PART TWO

Each age- or grade- level group will process through Chapter 16 in the student books. Here is an overview of the faith concepts and Disciple Power virtue for each grade.

GRADE 1 Chapter 16: Jesus Shows God's Love
Jesus saw people were hungry and gave them enough to eat; Jesus showed people that God cares for them, and he teaches us to care for people.
Disciple Power: wisdom

GRADE 2 Chapter 16: We Live as Disciples of Jesus
At the end of Mass, we receive God's blessing to live as Jesus' disciples; we go forth to glorify God and are a people sent on a mission.
Disciple Power: courage

GRADE 3 Chapter 16: Called to Serve
Bishops and priests lead people in worshiping God; men and women called to imitate Jesus in special ways are part of the consecrated life.
Disciple Power: wisdom

GRADE 4 Chapter 16: Signs of God's Love
The Sacraments at the Service of Communion set aside members of the Church to help others live holy lives.
Disciple Power: holiness

GRADE 5 Chapter 16: The Sacrament of Matrimony
Matrimony unites a baptized man and woman in a lifelong bond of faithful love; in their daily life a married couple serves each other, its family, and others with love.
Disciple Power: humility

GRADE 6 Chapter 16: Matrimony
Marriage is part of God's plan for love and life in which a man and a woman form a lifelong bond with openness to life; Matrimony is a living sign of God's love for the Church.
Disciple Power: chastity

WE REMEMBER

- Invite each group to present the one activity they have chosen to share from their chapters.

- Have each group present its Disciple Power virtues. Continue making the Disciple Power collage by adding today's virtues to it.

- If time permits, play Name that Faith Word (see page 34).

WE PRAY

- Choose the prayer from one of the grade level books from either Chapter 15 or Chapter 16 to pray together as a large group. Or use the following prayer.

- Dim the lights in the room, and replay the slideshow in the background during the prayer.

Light a candle and pray together the Sign of the Cross.

Leader: *Invite the children to spend a moment praying for Christ's light in their lives, then ask them to echo after you as you pray the following:*

Lord, help me to be a doer, not a talker.
Help me to say "It can be done," not "It can't be done."
Help me to improve, not merely disapprove.
Help me to get into the thick of things, not just sit on the sidelines.
Help me to point out what's right with the world, not always what's wrong.
Help me to light candles, not blow them out.
Lord, fill my heart with hope that looks for good in people,
    with hope that discovers what can be done,
    with hope that pushes ahead,
    with hope that opens doors,
    with hope that carries on.
Amen!
(Father James Keller, The Christophers)

Leader: God, Creator of the sun and moon and stars, you brought light to the darkness through your Son, Jesus Christ. May we always share Christ's light with others.
All: Amen.

 End today's prayer with "Christ Be Our Light" from the *Be My Disciples* Music Program, Grade 2 CD.

TO TAKE HOME

Remind the catechists and group leaders to have the children take home the Chapter Review and With My Family page from Chapters 15 and 16 to share with their families.

Give Glory to God

. . . .

"So whether you eat or drink, or whatever you do, do everything for the glory of God."

(1 Corinthians 10:31)

Background

As followers of Jesus we know that the darkness of death and sin is always present in the world. We also know that the glory of God is present all around us. We witness it through the words and actions of others, and we give others a glimpse of it by what we say and do.

We have received the Gifts of the Holy Spirit. They fill us with faith in Jesus, hope in eternal life, and constant love for God and for one another. We use our gifts to make the world a better place.

In Today's Session ... Enrichment activities will reinforce and enrich the children's learning of the past week, and they will celebrate Mass together as a learning community.

Getting Started
In Advance

❏ Day 10 includes a celebration of Mass at the end of the session. Schedule a celebrant for the Mass well ahead of time. A Liturgy Planning Worksheet for the Summer Program is available at *BeMyDisciples*.com in the section for Program Directors. (If you choose not to include a Mass, simply organize additional activities for the Activity Centers and Interactive Gallery.)

❏ Schedule a time with your catechists to plan for this session. As on Day 5, on Day 10 the children will participate in hands-on, interactive learning activities focused around their chapter learning, Catholic Social Teaching, and Liturgical Year lessons. They will also prepare to celebrate Mass in their small groups using the We Celebrate Mass section of the student books (see page 396 in the Catechist Guide). You will want to include your catechists in the planning of these activities.

❏ If you have chosen the Friday afternoon/evening option for Day 5, Day 10, and Day 15 with a potluck community meal, be sure to send out reminders to the families and larger community with details about the time, the place, and the potluck meal.

My Planning Notes
DAY 10

_____

_____

_____

_____

_____

_____

_____

❏ Determine the Activity Center format. You can plan age- or grade- level activities using the smaller meeting spaces for each grade, or you can organize the large group meeting space as a Learning Center where the children rotate in small groups from one activity to the next.

❏ Determine the number of activities and leadership you will need for today's session.

- The number of activities you choose will depend on the number of participants in your program, and the leadership available to facilitate the activities. Consider asking youth from the parish to help set up and facilitate the day's activities.

- Consider whether to organize the activities by grade level or by age- level groupings (primary, intermediate, or older children). Catechists from several grades can work together. You can plan a mix of age-specific activities and multi-age activities.

❏ Choose which learning activities will be a part of the interactive learning center. Refer to the grids on pages 90 and 91 for an overview of the many activities to choose from.

- Plan enough activities to fill a one-hour time frame. Choose activities best suited for your group. Some are suitable for all grade levels, some would work for age- level groups, and yet others would work nicely with older children helping the younger children. The Enriching the Lesson, Catholic Social Teaching, and Liturgical Year lessons work well as presented in the Catechist Guides, but the catechists can also use them as a starting point for their own creativity.

- The key is to aim for variety, creativity, and a bit of fun. Include a mix of language and music-related activities, person-related activities, and object-related activities. For more information and examples of each type, refer to 8 Kinds of Smart on page 27 in the Catechist Guide, and Activity Ideas on pages 18-19 in this manual. With your catechists, review and choose from the following:

Enriching the Lesson. Choose from the activities that appear at the end of Chapters 9 through 16 in the Catechist Guides, or create and plan similar types of activities. Choose activities related to the Eucharist, if possible. (See a listing of the Enriching the Lesson Activities on page 91.)

Catholic Social Teaching. Choose from activities that appear on page 195 (Unit 3: Dignity of Work and the Rights of Workers), and page 247 (Unit 4: Option for the Poor and Vulnerable) in the Catechist Guides. (See a listing on page 90.)

The Liturgical Year. Because today's session includes Mass, include the Triduum/ Holy Thursday activities (see page 378-379 in the Catechist Guides). Also consider: Ash Wednesday, Lent, Palm Sunday of the Passion of the Lord, Triduum/Good Friday, and Triduum/Easter. Choose from the lessons that appear on pages 372- 383 in the Catechist Guides.

❑ Decide how the children will process through the activities. Will you form small age- or grade- level groups that will travel together through the activities? Will you allow the children to choose from among the activities?

❑ Set up the large group meeting space.

• For the icebreaker Tic Tac Toe game, use masking tape to create a tic tac toe board at least 6 ft. by 6 ft. in size. Write X's on sheets of construction paper and O's on additional sheets.

• Post the We Worship wall and the Disciple Power collage somewhere in the large group meeting space where all can see them.

• Set up the Interactive Gallery or showcase space where the children will display their work (arts and crafts, worksheets, etc.), and where they will present (if applicable) role-plays, puppet shows, stories, or skits.

• Plan the Mass. Use the Liturgy Planning Worksheet available at *BeMyDisciples*.com in the section for Program Directors.

❑ Gather materials for all of the activities.

❑ If you have not already done so, collect one set of Faith Vocabulary/Faith Words cards from each age- or grade- level group for the eight chapters studied this week (Chapters 9 – 16). You will use these in the Get Focused activity.

AT A GLANCE CATHOLIC SOCIAL TEACHING

Catholic Social Teaching Activities	Unit Three, page 195	Unit Four, page 247
Grade 1	❑ Thanking Our Families	❑ Gift Bags for the Poor
Grade 2	❑ Showcasing the Work of Our Family	❑ Bread for the Poor
Grade 3	❑ Celebrating Those Who Give to Others	❑ Helping a Parish Mission Group
Grade 4	❑ Exploring Christian Vocation	❑ Helping Hurting Families
Grade 5	❑ Making Flash Cards for a Young Class	❑ Circle of Care
Grade 6	❑ The Dignity of the Disciple	❑ An Advice Column for Families

AT A GLANCE DAY 10

CHAPTERS 9 - 16

Enriching the Lesson Activities	Chapter 9, page 159	Chapter 10, page 174	Chapter 11, page 183	Chapter 12, page 195	Chapter 13, page 211	Chapter 14, page 223	Chapter 15, page 235	Chapter 16, page 247
Grade 1	☐ Singing Songs about the Church ☐ Playing a Game: What Season Am I? ☐ Literature Connection	☐ Making Lighted Candles ☐ Singing a Baptism Song ☐ Role-playing Baptism	☐ Reporting the Good News ☐ Drawing What Christians Do ☐ Building a Faith Vocabulary	☐ Drawing Family Portraits ☐ Literature Connection	☐ Learning a Walking Prayer ☐ Creating a Thank You Mural ☐ Literature Connection	☐ Making Forgiveness Bugs ☐ Role-playing Forgiveness ☐ Literature Connection	☐ Developing Good Listening Skills ☐ Praying for Others ☐ Literature Connection	☐ Making Fish Symbols ☐ Literature Connection
Grade 2	☐ Making Sacrament Booklets ☐ Retelling Scripture Stories ☐ Preparing Skits about Love for God	☐ Continuing Sacrament Booklets ☐ Staging a Baptism Role-Play ☐ Literature Connection	☐ Continuing Sacrament Booklets ☐ Creating a Collage of Gifts ☐ Literature Connection	☐ Using Puppets to Learn Forgiveness ☐ Continuing Sacraments Booklets	☐ Role-Playing Entrance Procession ☐ Continuing Sacraments Booklets ☐ Learning an Entrance Hymn	☐ Role-Playing Liturgy of the Word ☐ Continuing Sacraments Booklets ☐ Literature Connection	☐ Completing Sacraments Booklets ☐ A Blessing to Thank God ☐ Literature Connection	☐ Drawing the Last Supper ☐ Reinforcing Faith Vocabulary
Grade 3	☐ Take a Nature Walk ☐ Performing a Gospel Skit ☐ Literature Connection	☐ Creating Liturgical Movement ☐ Celebrating the Triduum ☐ Literature Connection	☐ Reviewing through Music ☐ Making Sacraments Booklets ☐ Literature Connection	☐ Making Sacraments Booklets ☐ Literature Connection	☐ Listening to God's Word ☐ Creating Storybooks ☐ Greeting Others at Mass	☐ Creating a Eucharist Senses Chart ☐ Continuing Sacraments Booklets ☐ Literature Connection	☐ Writing a Letter to a Married Couple ☐ Continuing Sacrament Booklets ☐ Literature Connection	☐ Completing Sacraments Booklets ☐ Literature Connection
Grade 4	☐ Using Scripture in Prayer ☐ Paraphrasing the Creed ☐ Miming a Teaching of Jesus	☐ Making Seasonal Banners ☐ Developing Word Games ☐ Role-Play: Greeters at Mass	☐ Sending Cards to Candidates for Sacraments of Initiation ☐ Baking Bread ☐ Adding to the Prayer Area	☐ Designing a TV Show ☐ Exploring States of Life	☐ Scripture Story Dioramas ☐ Bread for Others ☐ Kind Words and Actions Skits	☐ Forgiveness Interview ☐ Creating Scenarios ☐ Storytelling About Forgiveness	☐ Making Cards and Games for Children Who Are Ill ☐ Researching Messages for Cards ☐ Creating a Class Emblem	☐ Creating Rhythmic Messages about Holiness ☐ Making domestic Church Scrapbooks
Grade 5	☐ Role-Playing A Minister of Hospitality ☐ Creating a Liturgical Dance ☐ Making Sacraments Booklets	☐ Continuing Sacraments Booklets ☐ Designing Church Membership Cards ☐ Making Dioramas	☐ Continuing Sacraments Booklets ☐ Acting Out a Gift of the Holy Spirit ☐ Creating Profiles	☐ Creating a Bread of Life Collage ☐ Writing an Acrostic	☐ Continuing Sacraments Booklets ☐ Making Acrostic Poems ☐ Role-Playing a Story	☐ Continuing Sacraments Booklets ☐ Role-Playing a Scripture Story ☐ Making Banners for Sick Children	☐ Continuing Sacraments Booklets ☐ Role-Playing God's Call of Samuel ☐ Identifying Our Talents	☐ Continuing Sacraments Booklets ☐ Making Marriage Cards
Grade 6	☐ Creating Greetings of Joy ☐ Designing Symbols for Sacraments ☐ Making a Liturgical Season Mural	☐ Making Oral Presentations ☐ Creating Welcome-to-Church Cards ☐ Creating Faith Family Trees	☐ Writing an Advice Column ☐ Creating Acrostics ☐ Defining True Followers of Christ	☐ Creating Worship Aids ☐ Designing a Web Page for Living the Eucharist	☐ Writing in Journals ☐ Designing Reconciliation Guides ☐ Creating Scenarios about Forgiveness	☐ Creating Healing Songs ☐ Writing in Journals ☐ Illustrating a Book	☐ Planning a Multi-Media Presentation ☐ Charting and Comparing Works of Service ☐ Searching the Bible	☐ Developing a Television Pilot ☐ Writing Diamantes

Materials

- ❏ Bible, candle, cross, cloth for prayer space
- ❏ Materials for activities in the Learning Center
- ❏ CD player and *Be My Disciples* Music CD
- ❏ Set of Faith Vocabulary/Faith Words cards from each group
- ❏ Optional: Assign someone to be the photographer or videographer for the Be My Disciples Digital Scrapbook (see pages 18-19). Set up the digital scrapbook to be showing as the children enter the session.

WELCOME

Greet the children, their parents, and other adults who are participating in today's session. You, their catechists and helpers should be on hand to greet them when they arrive. This will help them feel safe and ready to participate.

ICEBREAKER

- Invite all of the children to gather in the large meeting space.

- Play Tic Tac Toe (see Day 5 warm up). This time, ask team members questions based on the material covered during the We Worship week.

LET'S GET FOCUSED

- Using the set of Faith Vocabulary/Faith Words cards you have collected from each of the age- or grade- level groups, play a Jeopardy-style game with the large group. Draw a card, and read aloud the definition of the word that appears on one side of it. Volunteers can call out the correct word that corresponds to the definition. For example: "The Sacraments of Matrimony and Holy Orders are these." Response: "What are the Sacraments at the Service of Communion?" Be sure to call on both younger and older children.

- Call out some of the Disciple Power virtues that the children explored during the week's four sessions. (Refer to the collage posted in the meeting space.) Have them offer examples of concrete ways they have practiced the virtues.

- Tell the children that the theme of this session is "Give Glory To God." Give them a moment to think about evidence around them of the glory of God. Ask: What are some of the signs around us that show us that God exists? Invite several volunteers to share with the large group. Transition into the opening prayer.

Bless Us, Lord

- Ask the children to bow their heads, close their eyes for a brief moment, and remember that God is present with them, in this time and place.

 Play or sing "All Are Welcome" from the *Be My Disciples* Music Program, Grade 1, Grade 4, or Grade 6 CD.

- Pray together the Sign of the Cross.

- Invite a volunteer to read aloud 1 Corinthians 10:31 from the Bible.

- Pose this question: What other things can we do to show the glory of God to those around us today? Invite children to share their examples with partners.

- End with the prayer, followed by the Sign of the Cross.

God ever-present,
may our faith in Jesus
and our love for you
continue to help us
reveal the glory of God
to others.
May everything we do,
both the big things
and the little things,
give glory to you.
Amen.

DISCOVER, Part One

INTRODUCE

- Briefly review some of the major faith concepts that appear on the We Worship wall. Tell the children that today they will have the opportunity to express what they have learned thus far in art, crafts, storytelling, and other creative activities.

- Provide a brief orientation for the session. During this orientation you can describe the various learning activities and how the children will process through them. Tell them that in the second part of the session they will prepare for and celebrate Mass.

TEACH, REINFORCE, CONNECT

- Invite the children to join their learning groups. Their catechists and leaders will be their guides as they travel through the activity stations.

- Allow approximately one hour for the children to visit the activity stations.

- Have the children bring the art, crafts, worksheets, etc. that they worked on during the first part of the session to their grades' section of the Interactive Gallery before moving into the break.

LET'S TAKE A BREAK!

When the age- or grade- level groups have completed their activities in DISCOVER, Part One, invite them to join together with all of the children in the program for refreshments and play time. (Note: Some groups may finish before others. To avoid distractions for the groups still meeting, if possible, set up the Break Time activities away from the meeting spaces.)

DISCOVER, Part Two

INTRODUCE

Note: This second part of the Day 10 session includes preparation for and celebration of Mass. If you are unable to include the celebration of Mass as a part of the program, simply continue the Activity Center process, and end with the Interactive Gallery presentations as on Day 5 (see page 27).

- Invite all of the children to gather in the large group meeting space with their learning groups. Tell them that they are now going to focus on preparing to celebrate Mass together as a group.

- Either in their age- or grade- level learning groups, or together as a large group, facilitate the We Celebrate the Mass material that appears in each of the student books (beginning on page 396 in the Catechist Guide). Encourage the catechists to take their children on a tour of the parish church. Alternatively, use the Tour of the Church activity on *BeMyDisciples*.com.

LET'S WRAP IT UP!

- Invite children and their families to visit the day's Interactive Gallery.
- Have the children sign the We Worship wall.
- Option: Show the Be My Disciples Digital Scrapbook during this time.

CONCLUSION

- Gather as a large group to practice sung Mass parts in preparation for the celebration of Mass.

 Choose from and practice the parts of the Mass that are in the *Be My Disciples* Music Program on the grade level CDs.

- Celebrate Mass together.

- Host a potluck meal for the community (optional).

Be My Disciples Week Three Overview

WEEK THREE: We Live

Background

In Christ we find a perfect blueprint for combining love of God and love of neighbor in a life that balances prayer with action. When we put the principles of Catholic morality into practice, we have a blueprint for the true happiness and success that Jesus describes in the Gospels. The Gifts of the Holy Spirit fill us with faith in Jesus, hope in eternal life, and constant love for God and for one another. We use our gifts to make the world a better place.

During Week Three, the children will explore the fifth and sixth units of the *Be My Disciples* curriculum, We Live: Part One and We Live: Part Two. They will learn more about their call to holiness and about the model for the moral life, Jesus Christ. On the last day of the program (Day 15) the We Are Disciples event will give the children the opportunity to meet with and learn about the work of the disciples in your own parish and broader community.

KEY FAITH CONCEPTS

- The Beatitudes
- The Ten Commandments
- The Great Commandment
- The Law of Love
- The Our Father

The Church Teaches ...

The *National Directory for Catechesis* teaches:

"In Christ, God reveals how we human beings are to live our lives. God created human beings with the freedom to initiate and direct their own actions and to shape their own lives.... This human freedom does not, however, entitle the person to say or do just anything. Human beings are not fully self-sufficient. We are capable of sin.... The more one chooses to do what is good, the more free one becomes ...Freely choosing to do the good, to obey the universal and unchanging moral norms, in no way diminishes the freedom and dignity of the human person" (*NDC* 41A).

Further Reading and Reflection

For more on the teachings of the Catholic Church on Christian morality and life in Christ, see the *Catechism of the Catholic Church* 1619-2557, and *United Stated Catholic Catechism for Adults*, pages 307–457.

Days 11-14

Each four-hour session includes warm-up and focusing activities, prayer celebrations, and grade or age-level learning groups in which the children explore chapters from Unit 5 and Unit 6 in the *Be My Disciples* student book. The sessions include a break for fun and refreshments. Let's Wrap it Up includes presentations of activities, Disciple Power virtues, and closing prayer.

Week Three WE LIVE	Day 11 Put On Love	Day 12 Come, Follow Me	Day 13 Love Never Fails	Day 14 Love One Another	Day 15 Be My Disciples!
Scripture	Colossians 3:14	Luke 18:22	1 Corinthians 13:4–5, 7–8a	John 15:12	John 8:31
Faith Focus	•We are called to holiness and to "put on love".	•Jesus invites us to follow him and to be his disciples.	•As Jesus' disciples we are called to lives of love.	•As Jesus' disciples we are called to love one another.	•We respond to Jesus' invitation: Be My Disciples! Liturgical Year: Ascension, Pentecost Catholic Social Teaching: Life and dignity of the human person; Solidarity of the human family
Discover, Part One	Learning Groups • Chapter 17	Learning Groups • Chapter 19	Learning Groups • Chapter 21	Learning Groups • Chapter 23	Activity Centers •Enriching the Lesson •Catholic Social Teaching •Liturgical Year
Discover, Part Two	Learning Groups • Chapter 18	Learning Groups • Chapter 20	Learning Groups • Chapter 22	Learning Groups • Chapter 24	We Are Disciples Event •Guests from the parish community and broader community share how they live as Jesus' disciples.
Let's Wrap It Up	• Activity sharing • Disciple Power presentations	• Activity sharing • Disciple Power presentations	• Activity sharing • Disciple Power presentations	• Activity sharing • Disciple Power presentations	Interactive Gallery • Displays • Presentations • Potluck Meal *(Families and Parish Community invited)*

Day 15: CONCLUDING DAY On Day 15, the concluding day of the three-week program, the children will participate in Activity Centers during the first part of the session. You can plan these activities by choosing from the Enriching the Lesson, Catholic Social Teaching, and Liturgical Year lessons that appear in the Catechist Guides for Units 5 and 6.

We Are Disciples Event The Day 15 session includes a We Are Disciples event which draws on members of the parish community and broader community to share with the children how they live as disciples in the world. Invite members of your parish community and the broader community to share their ministries with the children.

Interactive Gallery Day 15 is also an opportunity for the Summer Program participants to share how they have grown in faith over the past three weeks in the Interactive Gallery. Invite parents, family members, and other parishioners to this event. If possible, close with a potluck meal. We encourage you to adapt and design this day's session to best fit the needs and resources of your group.

Put On Love

"[O]ver all these put on love, that is, the bond of perfection."
(Colossians 3:14)

Background

Christians model the gifts of faith, hope, and love. Christian identity is marked with these gifts of the Holy Spirit. People who live by faith show through their attitudes and actions that they are followers of Jesus. They hope and believe in eternal life, but offer loving service to those in need today. They thank and praise God, and they show compassion and forgiveness to their neighbors. As the children in your program have been doing, they pray and celebrate together, and they learn about God and the Church together. They love God, and they try to love their enemies. Christians are identified by their faith, hope, and capacity for love. They make every effort to "put on love."

In Today's Session ... In Chapters 17 and 18 of each of their grade levels the children will discover how: Christians show their love for one another; all people are to be honored and respected; God gives us the grace to live holy and happy lives; we are created with a body and soul and with the gifts of an intellect and a free will; the grace of God helps us live holy lives; and the Theological Virtues strengthen us to live lives of holiness. The children will learn faith concepts such as: the Ten Commandments and the Beatitudes; moral decisions help us live as followers of Jesus Christ; and our consciences help us to judge whether or not an act is good or evil. They will learn about Disciple Power virtues, explore ways people of faith have lived those virtues, and be challenged to make faith choices about ways they can be disciples of Jesus. Today's session will expand and enrich their understanding of what it means to "put on love."

Faith Focus

We are called to holiness, and to "put on love."

My Planning Notes
DAY 11

_____
_____
_____
_____
_____
_____
_____
_____
_____
_____

Getting Started

In Advance

☐ Check in with your catechists and learning group leaders.

- Review the day's schedule.

- Explain and assign responsibilities for the Welcome, Let's Take A Break, and Let's Wrap It Up activities and prayers.

- Address any age- or grade- level specific needs your catechists may have, including materials needed.

- Remind the catechists to choose with their children one activity from the day's chapters to present to the large group during Let's Wrap It Up. Remind them to choose a creative strategy for presenting the two Disciple Power virtues to the large group (see pages 20-21), and to leave a bit of time at the end of their second session to plan the presentation.

☐ Set up the large group meeting space.

☐ Create and post a We Live wall by taping several sheets of newsprint together on a wall or board. Write We Live in large letters at the top of the newsprint. If possible, leave this up in your meeting space during the rest of the week, or, if necessary, carefully remove and store for the next day.

☐ Prepare the prayer environment.

☐ Gather materials for large group activities. Make one or more sandwich signs that say LOVE on both sides (see Get Focused).

☐ Have leaders cut out the Disciple Power words each group will learn (from Chapters 17 and 18) using colorful construction paper. You will post these during the Let's Wrap It Up segment to continue the creation of a Disciple Power collage.

☐ Ask leaders to make a set of Faith Vocabulary/ Faith Words cards from the two chapters. You will use these cards during Day 15, and, if time permits, during the Let's Wrap It Up segment in today's session.

☐ Optional: Assign someone to be the photographer or videographer for the *Be My Disciples* Digital Scrapbook (See pages 18-19 for suggestions). Set up the digital scrapbook to be showing as the children enter the session.

Materials

☐ Bible, candle(s), cross, cloth for prayer space

☐ *Be My Disciples* student books

☐ Newsprint, markers, and tape

☐ CD player and *Be My Disciples* Music CD

☐ Optional: projector, screen for Digital Scrapbook

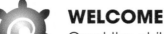

WELCOME

Greet the children. You and the catechists should be on hand to greet the children when they arrive, especially on this first day of the week. This will help them feel safe and ready to learn.

ICEBREAKER

- Invite all of the children to gather in the large meeting space.

- Play a large group icebreaker such as Simon Says. Include actions that invite the children to interact with each other, such as "Simon Says tell the person next to you what you did this past weekend," and so forth.

LET'S GET FOCUSED

- Have the children brainstorm some of the ordinary activities that are a part of being in a family…. neighborhood…. school…. group of friends…. team…. and so forth.

- Invite several volnteers to the front of the room. Give them an impromtu situation to role-play, such as family members arguing over whose turn it is to set the table, or feed the dog. Have them act it out, being as dramatic as they'd like. Then, bring out the sandwich signs you've made that say LOVE on them in big letters. Put these on one, two, or all volunteers. Say: Now that you have "put on love", re-enact the same situation.

- Repeat the role-plays (using different typical situations or ordinary, everyday situations where we need to "put on love") with other groups of volunteers. Invite the children to suggest situations for the role-plays, too. This will introduce the theme for the day.

Bless Us, Lord

- Ask the children to bow their heads, close their eyes for a brief moment, and remember that God is present with them in this time and place.

- Pray together the Sign of the Cross.

- Invite a child to read aloud Colossians 3:14 from Bible.

- Pose this question: In what way can we "put on love" while participating in today's activities? Invite the children to share their thoughts with their age- or grade- level groups.

- End with the prayer, followed by the Sign of the Cross.

Loving God,
you created us in
your own image and likeness.
Be with us and bless us
as we learn how to live
as your children.
Teach us what it
means to "put on love."
Amen.

 Sing "Ubi Caritas" from the *Be My Disciples* Music Program, Grades 2, 4, or 6 CD, to begin and end the prayer.

 DISCOVER, Part One

INTRODUCE

- Briefly describe the overall schedule for the day. Share any housekeeping information.

- Facilitate a large group brainstorming in response to this question: What words and phrases describe the actions and behaviors of people who are trying to live as Jesus' disciples?

- Write the words and phrases the children offer on the We Live wall.

- Tell them that today they will learn about how we are called to live as disciples of Jesus—how we are called to "put on love".

TEACH, REINFORCE, CONNECT

- Tell the children that they are now going to meet in their age- or grade- level groups.

- Invite the catechists to gather their children, and proceed to their assigned rooms.

- Allow groups to meet for approximately one hour.

AT A GLANCE PART ONE

Each age- or grade- level group will process through Chapter 17 in the student books using the Explore, Discover, and Decide methodology of the *Be My Disciples* curriculum. Here is an overview of the faith concepts and Disciple Power virtue for each grade. Groups will share a creative presentation of their Disciple Power virtues in the Let's Wrap It Up activity.

GRADE 1 Chapter 17: The First Christians
Christians believe in Jesus Christ and try to do what he taught; Christians today show their love for one another just as the first Christians did.
Disciple Power: understanding

GRADE 2 Chapter 17: In God's Image
All people are to be honored and respected; Jesus taught that we are to live as children of God; the Holy Spirit helps us make choices to live as children of God.
Disciple Power: kindness

GRADE 3 Chapter 17: Happiness with God
God gives us the grace to share in his divine life and to live happy and holy lives; Jesus promised us the gift of eternal life and happiness in Heaven.
Disciple Power: piety

GRADE 4 Chapter 17: Created in God's Image
We are each created with a body and a soul; God gave us an intellect and free will to help us make good moral choices.
Disciple Power: prudence

GRADE 5 Chapter 17: Called to Holiness
When we live as images of God, we live truly holy lives; the grace of God helps us live holy lives.
Disciple Power: goodness

GRADE 6 Chapter 17: Our Call to Holiness
The Theological Virtues are gifts from God that strengthen us to live lives of holiness; the grace of the Holy Spirit helps us grow in holiness; living the Works of Mercy is a sign we are trying to live holy lives
Disciple Power: understanding

LET'S TAKE A BREAK!

When the age- or grade- level groups have completed their work with the first chapter for the day, invite them to join together with all of the children in the program for refreshments and play time. (Note: Some groups may finish before others. To avoid distractions for the groups still meeting, if possible, set up the break activities away from the meeting spaces.)

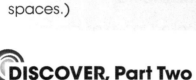

DISCOVER, Part Two

INTRODUCE

- Invite all of the children to gather in the large group meeting space with their learning groups.

- Direct their attention to the We Live wall. Going from group to group, ask the participants to name things they learned in their first sessions about how we live as Catholics.

- Write or have volunteers write responses on the newsprint.

TEACH, REINFORCE, CONNECT

- Tell the children that they are now going to meet again in their age- or grade- level groups to discover more about living as Catholics.

- Invite the catechists to proceed with their children to their classrooms or meeting rooms.

- Allow groups to meet for approximately 1 hour, 15 minutes.

AT A GLANCE PART TWO

Each age- or grade- level group will process through Chapter 18 in the student books. Here is an overview of the faith concepts and Disciple Power virtue for each grade.

GRADE 1 Chapter 18: We Love God
The Ten Commandments teach us to worship God; they teach us to speak God's name with love and respect and to take part in Mass on Sundays.
Disciple Power: knowledge

GRADE 2 Chapter 18: We Live as Children of God
Jesus teaches on his own authority; Jesus taught us the Great Commandment to love God and to love other people as we love ourselves.
Disciple Power: fortitude

GRADE 3 Chapter 18: God's Laws of Love
The First Commandment teaches us to love God above all else; the Second Commandment teaches us to love God by honoring his name; the Third Commandment teaches us to love God by keeping holy the Lord's Day.
Disciple Power: gentleness

GRADE 4 Chapter 18: The Beatitudes
God wants everyone to be blessed and truly happy; living the Beatitudes leads to happiness with God.
Disciple Power: generosity

GRADE 5 Chapter 18: Making Moral Decisions
Moral decisions help us grow as children of God and live as followers of Jesus Christ; conscience is our ability to know an judge what is right and what is wrong; the Cardinal Virtues help us live holy lives.
Disciple Power: prudence

GRADE 6 Chapter 18: Making Moral Choices
Sin is turning away from God; the sources of morality are the object of the act, the intention of the agent, and the circumstance surrounding the act; our conscience helps us judge whether an act is good or bad.
Disciple Power: prudence

LET'S WRAP IT UP!
REINFORCE

- Invite all of the children to gather, with their catechists, in the main meeting space.

- Direct everyone's attention once again to the We Live wall. Going from group to group, ask the participants to name things they learned in their second session about how Catholics are to live.

- Write or have volunteers write responses on the newsprint.

- Summarize the learning for the large group.

- Collect the extra set of Faith Vocabulary/Faith Words cards that each group has made.

WE REMEMBER

- Invite each group to present the one activity they have chosen to share from their chapters.

- Have each group present its Disciple Power virtues. Continue making the Disciple Power collage by adding today's virtues to it.

- If time permits, play Name that Faith Word (see page 34).

WE PRAY

- Choose the prayer from one of the grade level books from either Chapter 17 or Chapter 18 to pray together as a large group. Or use the following prayer ritual.

- Gather for prayer. If your group is large, have the children gather with their smaller learning groups. Each group will need a candle. (As an alternative, use crosses.)

We Pray

 Begin today's prayer with "Blest Are We" from the *Be My Disciples* Music Program, Grade 4 or Grade 6 CD.

Light the candles and pray together the Sign of the Cross.

Reader: (Read aloud Colossians 3:14.)

Pass the candle from one person to another. As each person holds the candle, the rest of the group says,

[Name], may you grow in holiness and live as a child of God. Put on love.

The person holding the candle responds, **Amen.**

Leader: God, help us to live as your children and to put on love. We ask this through Christ our Lord.

All: Amen.

TO TAKE HOME

Remind the catechists and group leaders to have the children take home the Chapter Review and With My Family page from Chapters 17 and 18 to share with their families.

Come, Follow Me

"…[C]ome, follow me."
(Luke 18:22)

Background

When we are baptized into Christ, we become adopted sons and daughters of God. We receive the gift of the Holy Spirit and the grace to live our new life in Christ. In union with Jesus and empowered by the Holy Spirit, we can love one another as Jesus commanded. Christian discipleship is rooted in the Law of Love taught by Jesus' words and example.

We receive the grace to live our new life in Christ, and we need to accept and respond to that grace. We have to freely choose to follow Christ. This is not a one-time decision. Choosing to follow Christ is a decision that must be made many times each day, day in and day out. As disciples of Jesus Christ, we are challenged to profess our faith in God through both our words and actions.

In Today's Session … In Chapters 19 and 20 of each of their grade levels the children will explore faith concepts such as: all people are children of God; the first three Commandments teach us to love and honor God; the last seven Commandments teach us how to love and respect ourselves and others; conscience and the virtues help us make good moral choices; the Gifts of the Holy Spirit help us; we are a Covenant people; Jesus is the new and everlasting Covenant; and what the Law of the Love demands of us. They will learn about the Great Commandment and discover that we live the Covenant when we love God with our whole hearts. They will learn about Disciple Power virtues, explore ways people of faith have lived the virtues, and be challenged to make faith choices about ways they can be a disciple of Jesus.

Faith Focus
Jesus invites us to follow him and to be his disciples.

My Planning Notes
DAY 12

_____
_____
_____
_____
_____
_____
_____
_____
_____
_____

Getting Started

In Advance

❏ Check in with your catechists and learning group leaders.

- Review the day's schedule.

- Explain and assign responsibilities for the Welcome, Let's Take A Break, and Let's Wrap It Up activities and prayers.

- Address any age- or grade- level specific needs your catechists may have, including materials needed.

- Remind the catechists to choose with their children one activity from the day's chapters to present to the large group during Let's Wrap It Up. Remind them to choose a creative strategy for presenting the two Disciple Power virtues to the large group (see pages 20-21), and to leave a bit of time at the end of their second session to plan the presentation.

❏ Set up the large group meeting space.

❏ Post the We Live wall if it is not already up.

❏ Prepare the prayer environment.

❏ Gather materials for large group activities.

❏ Have leaders cut out the Disciple Power words each group will learn (from Chapters 19 and 20) using colorful construction paper. You will post these during the Let's Wrap It Up segment to continue the creation of a Disciple Power collage.

❏ Ask leaders to make a set of Faith Vocabulary/Faith Words cards from the two chapters. You will use these cards during Day 15, and, if time permits, during the Let's Wrap It Up segment in today's session.

❏ Optional: Assign someone to be the photographer or videographer for the *Be My Disciples* Digital Scrapbook (see pages 18-19). Set up the digital scrapbook to be showing as the children enter the session.

Materials

❏ Bible, candle, cross, cloth for prayer space

❏ *Be My Disciples* student books

❏ Newsprint, markers, and tape

❏ Paper and pens or pencils

❏ CD player and *Be My Disciples* Music CD

❏ Optional: projector, screen for Digital Scrapbook

WELCOME

You and the catechists should be on hand to greet the children when they arrive. This will help them feel safe and ready to learn.

ICEBREAKER

- Invite all of the children to gather in the meeting space.

- Play a large group icebreaker such as "Find Somebody Who". In this game, older children partner with the younger children to search for people in the group who meet certain criteria on a list you provide. For example, "Find somebody who lives on the same street as your or your partner." "Find somebody who is born in the same month as one of you." "Find somebody whose last name begins with the first letter of you or your partner's first name." Create a list of criteria based on what you know about the children. Write your list on newsprint and post, numbering the criteria 1 through 10. Give each set of partners a piece of paper and pen or pencil. Have them number down the left margin 1 through 10. When they find someone who meets the criteria, that person signs the corresponding number on the pair's paper. Which pair can be the first to find people who fit all ten criteria? Consider having small prizes, such as prayer cards, bookmarks, or crosses, for the pairs who finish first, second, and third.

LET'S GET FOCUSED

- Ask the children to sit with their learning group. Then ask them to imagine that Jesus has just come and joined their group. He sits down with them and says, "Come, follow me." Ask the children to talk about what their responses to his invitation would be. What would the conversation with Jesus be like? What questions would they want to ask Jesus about what it means to follow him? What do they think Jesus would say?

- Invite volunteers to share with the large group highlights of their small group discussion.

- Share the following: In the Gospel, Jesus said to his followers, "Come, follow me." Suggest to the children that they are learning what it means to follow Jesus. In today's session, they will explore loving God and loving others.

Bless Us, Lord

- Ask the children to bow their heads, close their eyes for a brief moment, and remember that God is present with them in this time and place.

- Pray together the Sign of the Cross.

- Invite a volunteer to say aloud today's Scripture verse from Luke 18:22: "…[C]ome, follow me."

- Pose this question: Jesus says "Come, follow me." How do you respond?

    - Play "We are Called" from the *Be My Disciples* Music Program, Grade 4 or Grade 6 CD, while the children reflect.

- End with the prayer, followed by the Sign of the Cross.

Loving God, be with us and bless us as we seek to respond to your Son, Jesus' invitation, "Come, follow me". Amen.

DISCOVER, Part One

INTRODUCE

- Briefly describe the overall schedule for the day. Share any housekeeping information..

- Point out the We Live wall to reinforce the learning from the previous day.

AT A GLANCE PART ONE

Each age- or grade- level group will process through Chapter 19 in the student books using the Explore, Discover, and Decide methodology of the *Be My Disciples* curriculum. Here is an overview of the faith concepts and Disciple Power virtue for each grade. Groups will share about their Disciple Power virtues in the large group Let's Wrap It Up activity.

GRADE 1 Chapter 19: We Love Others
We are to treat ourselves and others as children of God; we are to show respect for other people and tell the truth.
Disciple Power: temperance

GRADE 2 Chapter 19: We Love God
God gave us the Ten Commandments to live happy lives; the first three Commandments teach us to love God.
Disciple Power: obedience

GRADE 3 Chapter 19: Love One Another
The last seven Commandments teach us how to love and respect others and ourselves; they teach us to be honest and truthful, kind and generous.
Disciple Power: self-control

GRADE 4 Chapter 19: Living a Holy Life
Conscience and the virtues helps us make good moral choices; sin is freely choosing to say or do something we know is against God's will; the Gifts of the Holy Spirit help us choose to live as followers of Jesus.
Disciple Power: justice

GRADE 5 Chapter 19: Living the Covenant
We are a Covenant people; God gave Moses the Ten Commandments to guide us in living the Covenant; Jesus, the Son of God is the new and everlasting Covenant.
Disciple Power: obedience

GRADE 6 Chapter 19: The Law of Love
Principles of the natural law; love of God and love of neighbor is essentially the Great Commandment; the Law of Love is the way we are called to be friends with Jesus and with one another.
Disciple Power: charity

TEACH, REINFORCE, CONNECT

- Tell the children that they are now going to meet in their age- or grade- level groups to discover more about how we live as Catholics.

- Invite the catechists to gather their children, and proceed to their classrooms or meeting rooms.

- Allow groups to meet for approximately one hour.

LET'S TAKE A BREAK!

When the age- or grade- level groups have completed their work with the first chapter for the day, invite them to join together with all of the children in the program for refreshments and play time. (Note: Some groups may finish before others. To avoid distractions for the groups still meeting, if possible, set up the break activities away from the meeting spaces.)

DISCOVER, Part Two

INTRODUCE

- Invite all of the children to gather in the large group meeting space with their learning groups.

- Direct their attention to the We Live wall. Going from group to group, ask the participants to name things they learned in their first session about how Catholics follow Jesus.

- Write or have volunteers write responses on the newsprint.

TEACH, REINFORCE, CONNECT

- Tell the children that they are now going to meet again in their age- or grade- level groups to discover more about how we live as Catholics.

- Invite the catechists to proceed with their children to their classrooms or meeting rooms.

- Allow groups to meet for approximately 1 hour, 15 minutes.

AT A GLANCE PART TWO

Each age- or grade- level group will process through Chapter 20 in the student books. Here is an overview of the faith concepts and Disciple Power virtue for each grade.

GRADE 1 Chapter 20: We Live as a Community
The Great Commandment teaches us to love God and to love others as we love ourselves and to live as good members of the community.
Disciple Power: justice

GRADE 2 Chapter 20: We Love Others
People who live the Ten Commandments help build a kind world; Jesus calls us to follow him by keeping the Ten Commandments and the Golden Rule.
Disciple Power: justice

GRADE 3 Chapter 20: The Great Commandment
We live the Covenant when we love God with our whole hearts and when we love other people as we love ourselves.
Disciple Power: prudence

GRADE 4 Chapter 20: Living God's Covenant
The Ten Commandments teach us how to love God and our neighbors as ourselves; Jesus came to show us how to live the Ten Commandment.
Disciple Power: fortitude

GRADE 5 Chapter 20: The Beatitudes
The Beatitudes show ways Jesus wants his disciples to live; they describe the qualities and actions of people blessed by God.
Disciple Power: justice

GRADE 6 Chapter 20: Ways of Happiness
The Beatitudes are teachings of Jesus from the Sermon on the Mount; living the Beatitudes is the way to follow the Law of Love.
Disciple Power: joy

LET'S WRAP IT UP!

REINFORCE

- Invite all of the children to gather, with their groups and catechists, in the main meeting space.

- Direct everyone's attention once again to the We Live wall. Going from group to group, ask the participants to name things they learned in their second session about how Catholics follow Jesus.

- Write or have volunteers write responses on the newsprint.

- Summarize the learning for the large group.

- Collect the extra set of Faith Vocabulary/Faith Words cards that each group has made.

WE REMEMBER

- Invite each group to present the one activity they have chosen to share from their chapters.

- Have each group present its Disciple Power virtues. Continue making the Disciple Power collage by adding today's virtues to it.

- If time permits, play Name that Faith Word (see page 34).

WE PRAY

- Choose the prayer from one of the grade level books from either Chapter 19 or Chapter 20 to pray together as a large group. Or use the following prayer ritual.

- Gather the participants for prayer. Tell them that the first followers of Jesus, the earliest Christians, were led by their faith in Jesus. They lived in service to the community. Serving others as Christ did is an ongoing, lifelong commitment that draws us closer to Christ.

We Pray

- Light a candle and pray together the Sign of the Cross.

Leader: God, our Creator, we are thankful for the time we have shared today. Help us respond to Jesus' invitation to follow him. Be with us as we pray together. Amen.

Reader: (Read aloud Acts of the Apostles 2:42-47.)

- Invite all who want to do so to say a prayer of petition, asking God to help them live their faith in Jesus as did the first Christians.

For example: **"Lord, help us share with each other."**

- After each person prays his or her petition, the rest of the group responds, **Lord, help us to follow you.**

- Close by joining hands and praying the Our Father aloud. Conclude by sharing a Sign of Peace.

 End today's prayer with "Your Grace is Enough" from the *Be My Disciples* Music Program, Grade 5 CD.

TO TAKE HOME

Remind the catechists and group leaders to have the children take home the Chapter Review and With My Family page from Chapters 19 and 20 to share with their families.

Love Never Fails

"Love is patient, love is kind. It is not jealous, [love] is not pompous, it is not inflated, it is not rude, . . . It bears all things, believes all things, hopes all things, endures all things. Love never fails."

(1 Corinthians 13: 4-5, 7-8a)

Background

Love is the motivating factor for those who would follow Jesus as his disciples. Loving one another is not always easy or simple. Jesus asks that his disciples look at the ways in which he loves them for the model of love. Jesus came to show all people how to love: with selfless concern and care for others. Jesus' model of loving service is one that Christians attempt to follow. In his life and his Death Jesus put the welfare of others before his own. He cared deeply for the oppressed, for outcasts, for children, for women, for sinners, and for all who struggle with the difficulties of human existence. He taught that God's love will overcome all injustice, evil, and suffering. This will happen only when believers begin to live out the true meaning of love—serving others as Jesus taught. God is love and he calls people to be all that they can be. Love never fails.

In Today's Session ... In Chapters 21 and 22 of each of the grade levels, the children will explore and learn faith concepts such as: God loves all people and desires for us to live with him in Heaven; making wise choices; the ministry of missionaries; and the first three Commandments teach us to love God. They will also learn: God created all people in his image; we are to take care of the gift of life; we make wise choices when we choose to live as Jesus taught; we profess what we believe in the creeds of the Church; the Fourth, Fifth, Sixth, and Ninth Commandments teach love and respect towards other people. They will learn about Disciple Power virtues, explore ways people of faith have lived those virtues, and be challenged themselves to make faith choices about ways they can be disciples of Jesus.

Faith Focus

As Jesus' disciples we are called to love God with all our hearts.

My Planning Notes
DAY 13

_____
_____
_____
_____
_____
_____
_____
_____
_____
_____

Getting Started

In Advance

❑ Check in with your catechists and learning group leaders.

- Review the day's schedule.

- Explain and assign responsibilities as needed for the Welcome, Let's Take A Break, and Let's Wrap It Up activities and prayers.

- Address any age- or grade- level specific needs your catechists may have, including materials needed.

- Remind the catechists to choose with their children one activity from the day's chapters to present to the large group during Let's Wrap It Up. Remind them to choose a creative strategy for presenting the two Disciple Power virtues to the large group (see pages 20-21), and to leave a bit of time at the end of their second session to plan the presentation.

❑ Set up the large group meeting space.

❑ Post the We Live wall.

❑ Prepare the prayer environment.

❑ Gather materials for large group activities. For closing prayer, prepare slips of paper that say "I will love by _____" on them.

❑ Have leaders cut out the Disciple Power words each group will learn (from Chapters 21 and 22) using colorful construction paper. You will post these during the Let's Wrap It Up segment to continue the creation of a Disciple Power collage.

❑ Ask leaders to make a set of Faith Vocabulary/Faith Words cards from the two chapters. You will use these cards during Day 15, and, if time permits, during the Let's Wrap It Up segment in today's session.

❑ Optional: Assign someone to be the photographer or videographer for the *Be My Disciples* Digital Scrapbook (see pages 18-19). Set up the digital scrapbook to be showing as the children enter the session.

Materials

❑ Bible, candle, cross, cloth for prayer space
❑ *Be My Disciples* student books
❑ Newsprint, markers, and tape
❑ Pens or pencils
❑ Foam ball for icebreaker
❑ CD player and *Be My Disciples* Music CD
❑ Optional: projector, screen for Digital Scrapbook

WELCOME

You and the catechists should be on hand to greet the children when they arrive. This will help them feel safe and ready to learn.

ICEBREAKER

- Invite all of the children to gather in the large meeting space.

- Play a large group icebreaker such as Toss the Ball. (See page 38.) Each time a child catches the ball, he or she fills in the blank: "Love is _____."

LET'S GET FOCUSED

- Ask the children to gather around the prayer table.

- Facilitate a large group "think, pair, share" process. First, invite the children to think about one way they have shown love or respect for others this week, and one way they have witnessed others show love or respect. Next, have them find a partner, and share in pairs experiences when they showed love and respect, and when they witnessed love and respect.

- Invite volunteers to share with the large group, and then begin the opening prayer.

Bless Us, Lord

- Ask the children to bow their heads, close their eyes for a brief moment, and remember that God is present with them in this time and place.

- Pray together the Sign of the Cross.

- Invite a child to read aloud 1 Corinthians 13: 4-5, 7-8a from the Bible.

- Pose this reflection question: How do we show that we love each other?

 • Play the "We Are Disciples" instrumental version from the *Be My Disciples* Music Program, all Grade level CDs, in the background during the reflection.

- End with the prayer, followed by the Sign of the Cross.

Loving God,
be with us
and bless us
as we seek to respond
to your Son, Jesus'
invitation to be
his disciples.
Help us love you
with all our hearts,
every minute
of the day.
Amen.

DISCOVER, Part One

INTRODUCE

- Briefly describe the overall schedule for the day. Share any housekeeping information.

- Invite responses to "To be a disciple of Jesus means _____." Write key words and phrases on the We Live wall.

TEACH, REINFORCE, CONNECT

- Tell the children that they are now going to meet in their age- or grade- level groups to discover more about what it means to be disciples of Jesus.

- Invite the catechists to gather their children, and proceed to their classrooms or meeting rooms.

- Allow groups to meet for approximately one hour.

AT A GLANCE PART ONE

Each age- or grade- level group will process through Chapter 21 in the student books using the Explore, Discover, and Decide methodology of the *Be My Disciples* curriculum. Here is an overview of the faith concepts and Disciple Power virtue for each grade. Groups will share about their Disciple Power virtues in the large group Let's Wrap It Up activity.

GRADE 1 Chapter 21: Jesus and the Children
God loves all people and wants all people to come to him. God wants us to live in Heaven.
Disciple Power: joy

GRADE 2 Chapter 21: We Make Choices
It is important to make wise choices that will help us find happiness; the Proverbs can help us choose wisely.
Disciple Power: humility

GRADE 3 Witnesses of Faith
Saul, who became known as Paul, was a disciple of Jesus; women disciples also accompanied Jesus and the Apostles; missionaries travel the world to help people come to know Jesus.
Disciple Power: reverence

GRADE 4 Chapter 21: Love God with All Your Heart
The First Commandment teaches us to worship only God; the Second Commandment teaches us to show our love and respect for all that belongs to God; the Third Commandment teaches that the Lord's Day is holy.
Disciple Power: diligence

GRADE 5 Chapter 21: Love of God
The First, Second, and Third Commandments describe our privilege and responsibility to worship God; the Lord's Day is a holy day; Sunday is the Lord's Day for Christians.
Disciple Power: meekness

GRADE 6 Chapter 21: Love of God
The First Commandment teaches us to worship only God; the Second Commandment teaches us to use the name of God reverently; the Third Commandment teaches us to keep the Lord's Day holy.
Disciple Power: piety

LET'S TAKE A BREAK!

When the age- or grade- level groups have completed their work with the first chapter for the day, invite them to join together with all of the children in the program for refreshments and play time. (Note: Some groups may finish before others. To avoid distractions for the groups still meeting, if possible, set up the Let's Take a Break activities away from the meeting spaces.)

DISCOVER, Part Two

INTRODUCE

- Invite all of the children to gather in the large group meeting space with their learning groups.

- Direct their attention to the We Live wall. Going from group to group, ask the participants to name things they learned in their first session about how Catholics live as disciples of Jesus.

- Write or have volunteers write responses on the newsprint

TEACH, REINFORCE, CONNECT

- Tell the children that they are now going to meet again in their age- or grade- level groups to discover more about living as Catholics.

- Invite the catechists to proceed with their children to their classrooms or meeting rooms.

- Allow groups to meet for approximately 1 hour, 15 minutes.

AT A GLANCE PART TWO

Each age- or grade- level group will process through Chapter 22 in the student books. Here is an overview of the faith concepts and Disciple Power virtue for each grade.

GRADE 1 Chapter 22: We Are Children of God
God created all people in his image; God gives us the gift of life; we are to take care of the gift of life.
Disciple Power: gentleness

GRADE 2 Chapter 22: We Can Choose Right from Wrong
We make wise choices when we choose to live as Jesus taught; we use our consciences to make wise choices; all of our choices have consequences.
Disciple Power: joy

GRADE 3 Chapter 22: The Creeds
We profess what we believe about God in the creeds; praying the creeds of the Church helps us grow as a Church family.
Disciple Power: knowledge

GRADE 4 Chapter 22: Love Your Neighbor as Yourself
The Fourth Commandment teaches about our responsibilities towards our families; the Fifth Commandment teaches us to respect and honor life; the Sixth and Ninth Commandments teach us to express our love and friendships in appropriate ways.
Disciple Power: respect

GRADE 5 Chapter 22: Love of Neighbor
The Fourth Commandment teaches us to obey and respect our parents; the Fifth Commandment teaches us to respect all human life as sacred; the Sixth and Ninth Commandments teach us to be chaste.
Disciple Power: temperance

GRADE 6 Chapter 22: Commandments of Love
The Fourth Commandment teaches about our responsibilities as family members and citizens; the Fifth Commandment teaches about a culture of life; the Sixth and Ninth Commandments
Disciple Power: temperance

LET'S WRAP IT UP!

REINFORCE

- Invite all of the children, with their catechists, to gather in the main meeting space.
- Direct everyone's attention once again to the We Live wall. Going from group to group, ask the participants to name things they learned in their second session about living as Catholics.
- Write or have volunteers write responses on the newsprint.
- Summarize the learning for the large group.
- Collect the extra set of Faith Vocabulary/Faith Words cards that each group has made.

WE REMEMBER

- Invite each group to present the one activity they have chosen to share from their chapters.
- Have each group present its Disciple Power virtues. Continue making the Disciple Power collage by adding today's virtues to it.
- If time permits, play Name that Faith Word (see page 34).

WE PRAY

- Invite each group to choose the closing prayer from one of the grade level books, Chapter 21 or Chapter 22 to pray together as a large group. Or use the following prayer ritual.

We Pray

Light a candle and pray together the Sign of the Cross.

Leader: Loving God, we are thankful for the time we have shared today. Be with us as we pray together.

Reader: (Read aloud 1 Corinthians 13:4-5, 7-8 from the Bible.)

Pass out the slips of paper that say "I will love by _____" and pencils to the children. Give them a few minutes of quiet to write down one way that they will show love to others today. Have the learning group leaders collect the papers in a basket and come forward to the prayer center.

Leader: Dear Lord, today we make the choice to love. Here are some of the ways we will do so.

Ask the learning group leaders to take turns drawing the slips of paper from their group's basket. Have them read aloud what is written on the papers. After each statement is read, the whole group responds, **"Love never fails."**

Leader: Love is patient.   **All:** Love never fails.

Leader: Love is kind.   **All:** Love never fails.

Leader: Love is not jealous.   **All:** Love never fails.

Leader: Love is not rude.   **All:** Love never fails.

Leader: Love rejoices in the truth. **All:** Love never fails.

Leader: Love bears all things, believes all things, hopes all things, endures all things.

All: Love never fails. Amen.

End today's prayer with "Go Make A Difference" from the *Be My Disciples* Music Program, Grade 6 CD.

TO TAKE HOME

Remind the catechists and group leaders to have the children take home the Chapter Review and With My Family page from Chapters 21 and 22 to share with their families.

Love One Another

"This is my commandment: love one another as I love you."

(John 15:12)

Background

If you were to conduct a detailed summary of Jesus' actions and words throughout his life, you would discover that service flowing out of love for his Father and for people underlies Jesus' work on Earth. Jesus Christ teaches not only through his preaching, but through all his words and deeds during his public ministry, his miracles, and most especially by the self-sacrificing love shown to us in his Paschal Mystery.

The Law of Love revealed by Christ was at the heart of the moral life of the early Church. As the Body of Christ, we are to be signs of God, who is love (see 1 John 4:6). In concrete, practical ways, we are to live Jesus' New Commandment.

In Today's Session ... In Chapters 23 and 24 of each of the grade levels, the children will explore and learn faith concepts such as: grace is a gift from God; the Beatitudes show ways Jesus wants his disciples to live; and the Seventh, Eighth and Tenth Commandments guide us in how love and respect others. The children will explore the Our Father. They will learn that Jesus invites us to address God the Father as Abba and to place our trust unconditionally in the Father as he himself did. They will learn about Disciple Power virtues, explore ways people of faith have lived them, and be challenged to make faith choices about ways they can be disciples of Jesus. The simple message for this lession, regardless of the children's grade level, is "love one another".

My Planning Notes
DAY 14

_____
_____
_____
_____
_____
_____
_____
_____
_____

Faith Focus

As Jesus' disciples we are called to love one another.

Getting Started

In Advance

❑ Check in with your catechists and learning group leaders.

- Review the day's schedule.

- Explain and assign responsibilities as needed for the Welcome, Let's Take A Break, and Let's Wrap It Up activities and prayers.

- Address any age- or grade- level specific needs your catechists may have, including materials needed.

- Remind the catechists to choose with their children one activity from the day's chapters to present to the large group during Let's Wrap It Up. Remind them to choose a creative strategy for presenting the two Disciple Power virtues to the large group (see pages 20-21), and to leave a bit of time at the end of their second session to plan the presentation.

❑ Set up the large group meeting space.

❑ Post the We the We Live wall if it is not already up

❑ Prepare the prayer environment.

❑ Gather materials for large group activities.

❑ Create a slideshow of images that depict light.

❑ Have leaders cut out the Disciple Power words each group will learn (from Chapters 23 and 24) using colorful construction paper. You will post these during the Let's Wrap It Up segment to continue the creation of a Disciple Power collage.

❑ Ask leaders to make a set of Faith Vocabulary/Faith Words cards from the two chapters. You will use these cards during Day 15, and, if time permits, during the Let's Wrap It Up segment in today's session.

❑ Optional: Assign someone to be the photographer or videographer for the *Be My Disciples* Digital Scrapbook (see pages 18-19). Set up the digital scrapbook to be showing as the children enter the session.

Materials

❑ Bible, candle, cross, cloth for prayer space
❑ *Be My Disciples* student books
❑ Newsprint, markers, and tape
❑ CD player and *Be My Disciples* Music CD
❑ Optional: projector, screen for Digital Scrapbook

WELCOME

You and the catechists should be on hand to greet the children when they arrive. This will help them feel safe and ready to learn.

ICEBREAKER

- Invite all of the children to gather in the large meeting space.

- Play a large group icebreaker such as Toss the Ball. (See page 38.) You can begin by repeating the same process as in the previous session (Love is ____). Then, call out a category or prompt such as "Name a Saint you have learned about this summer." Switch the prompt several times in the middle of the icebreaker.

LET'S GET FOCUSED

- Invite the children to join their catechists to form the program's age- or grade-level learning groups.

- Distribute a sheet of newsprint and marker to each group. Have the catechists write "Love one another" on their newsprints. Instruct the groups to create a word web or mind map around the sentence by adding words and phrases around it which define and describe what it means to "love one another."

- Invite the children to re-gather as a large group. Have the catechists or volunteers from each group present and post their newsprints.

- Talk briefly about their responses; even share a few of your own. Suggest that every day we can grow in our knowledge of who God is, experience how much he loves us, and learn how to best love him through how we live and how we serve others.

- Briefly describe the overall schedule for the day. Share any housekeeping information.

- Ask the children to bow their heads, close their eyes for a brief moment, and remember that God is present with them in this time and place.

- Pray together the Sign of the Cross.

- Invite a volunteer to read aloud John 15:12 from the Bible.

- Pose this question: What are some of the ways that we love each other? Invite volunteers to share with the large group.

- End with the prayer, followed by the Sign of the Cross.

Bless Us, Lord

Heavenly Father,

help us love and respect

all people as

our brothers and sisters.

In those times when it is

hard to do so,

help us to love

as you have loved us.

Amen.

DISCOVER, Part One

INTRODUCE

- Review the We Live wall.

- Invite the children to name ways they have seen others live as Jesus teaches us to live in the past week.

AT A GLANCE

Each age- or grade- level group will process through Chapter 23 in the student books using the Explore, Discover, and Decide methodology of the *Be My Disciples* curriculum. Here is an overview of the faith concepts and Disciple Power virtue for each grade. Groups will share about their Disciple Power virtues in the large group Let's Wrap It Up activity.

GRADE 1 Chapter 23: Jesus Teaches about Love
Jesus told the parable of the Good Samaritan to help us live as his followers; God wants us to care for others; we show charity when we love our neighbors.
Disciple Power: charity

GRADE 2 Chapter 23: We Share in God's Life
Sanctifying grace is a gift of God's life that he shares with us; the gift of peace helps us live happy and holy lives.
Disciple Power: trust

GRADE 3 Chapter 23: Living Our Faith
The Beatitudes show ways Jesus wants his disciples to live and tell us what happens to people who obey God's Laws.
Disciple Power: perseverance

GRADE 4 Chapter 23: Love One Another
The Seventh Commandment teaches respect for others' property; the Eighth Commandment teaches us to be honest and truthful; the Tenth Commandment teaches us to be grateful and generous.
Disciple Power: mercy

GRADE 5 Chapter 23: Living a Just and Truthful Life
The Seventh Commandment teaches us to not take what doesn't belong to us; the Eight Commandment teaches us to be truthful; the Tenth Commandment teaches good stewardship.
Disciple Power: integrity

GRADE 6 Chapter 23: Love of Neighbor
The Seventh and Tenth Commandments teach us to respect the resources God has given us and goods belonging to others; the Eighth Commandment teaches us to speak the truth; we use our talents for the common good.
Disciple Power: generosity

TEACH, REINFORCE, CONNECT

- Tell the children that they are now going to meet in their age- or grade- level groups to discover more about how Catholics live.

- Invite the catechists to gather their children, and proceed to their classrooms or meeting rooms.

- Allow groups to meet for approximately one hour.

LET'S TAKE A BREAK!

When the age- or grade-level groups have completed their work with the first chapter for the day, invite them to join together with all of the children in the program for refreshments and play time. (Note: Some groups may finish before others. To avoid distractions for the groups still meeting, if possible, set up the Break Time activities away from the meeting spaces.)

DISCOVER, Part Two

INTRODUCE

- Invite all of the children to gather in the large group meeting space with their learning groups.

- Direct their attention to the We Live wall. Going from group to group, ask the participants to name things they learned in their first session about how Catholics live.

- Write or have volunteers write responses on the newsprint.

TEACH, REINFORCE, CONNECT

- Tell the children that they are now going to meet again in their age- or grade-level groups to discover more about how Catholics live.

- Invite the catechists to proceed with their children to their classrooms or meeting rooms.

- Allow groups to meet for approximately 1 hour, 15 minutes.

AT A GLANCE PART TWO

Each age- or grade- level group will process through Chapter 24 in the student books. Here is an overview of the faith concepts and Disciple Power virtue for each grade.

GRADE 1 Chapter 24: The Our Father
Jesus taught us to pray the Our Father, the prayer of all Christians.
Disciple Power: humility

GRADE 2 Chapter 24: The Our Father
We show our love and adoration for God when we pray the Our Father; the Our Father helps us prepare for the Kingdom of God.
Disciple Power: hope

GRADE 3 Chapter 24: Praying as Jesus Did
Jesus taught us to talk and listen to God the Father; Jesus taught us to pray with trust.
Disciple Power: obedience

GRADE 4 Chapter 24: The Prayer of Disciples
Jesus is our Teacher who helps us live as children of God; Jesus taught us to call God Father; when we pray the Lord's Prayer we tell God that he is the center of our lives.
Disciple Power: charity

GRADE 5 Chapter 24: Lord, Teach Us to Pray
Jesus taught his disciples to pray the Our Father; the Our Father teaches us how to pray; the Our Father teaches us how to live the Gospel.
Disciple Power: piety

GRADE 6 Chapter 24: The Summary of the Gospel
The Lord's Prayer is the prayer of all Christians; it teaches us to live the Gospel.
Disciple Power: hope

LET'S WRAP IT UP!

REINFORCE

- Invite all of the children to gather, with their catechists, in the main meeting space.
- Direct everyone's attention once again to the We Live wall. Going from group to group, ask the participants to name things they learned in their second session about how Catholics are called to live.
- Write or have volunteers write responses on the newsprint.
- Summarize the learning for the large group.
- Collect the extra set of Faith Vocabulary/Faith Words cards that each group has made.

WE REMEMBER

- Invite each group to present the one activity they have chosen to share from their chapters.
- Have each group present its Disciple Power virtues. Continue making the Disciple Power collage by adding today's virtues to it.
- If time permits, play Name that Faith Word (see page 34).

WE PRAY

- Choose the prayer from one of the grade level books from either Chapter 23 or Chapter 24 to pray as a large group. Or use the following prayer ritual.

We Pray

Light a candle and pray together the Sign of the Cross.

Leader: Spirit of the Lord, lead us in prayer. Help us hear the voice of Jesus, who calls us to love one another. Amen.

- Invite the children to close their eyes as the Reader slowly and reflectively prays the Scripture passage.

Reader: (Read John 15:9-17, slowly and reverently.)

- Invite the children to offer Prayers of Petition.

Leader: Together, let us pray the prayer that Jesus taught us.

All: Our Father …

 End today's prayer with the song "Rain Down" from the *Be My Disciples* Music Program, Grade 2 CD.

TO TAKE HOME

Remind the catechists and group leaders to have the children take home the Chapter Review and With My Family page from Chapters 23 and 24 to share with their families.

Be My Disciples!

". . . If you remain in my word, you will truly be my disciples, and you will know the truth, and the truth will set you free."

(John 8:31)

Background

When we are baptized, we receive the same mission Jesus handed on to his disciples—*to be his disciples.* Through word and witness, we are called to share with others the faith that we have been given. During this Summer Program, you and your leadership team have lived out the ministry of evangelization in a special way by sharing the truths of the Catholic faith with the children.

Evangelization has been the work of the Church ever since Jesus commanded his Apostles to "Go into the world and proclaim the gospel to every creature" (Mark 16:15). Evangelization is sharing the Good News about God's loving plan of Salvation for all his children through the life, Passion, Death, Resurrection, and Ascension of Jesus Christ. Our first responsibility is to help children meet Jesus, not just in class sessions or in the liturgy, but also in their daily lives; that is, wherever faith is lived out. Faith in Jesus is inseparable from daily life. For a true disciple, only faith in Christ gives meaning to life. As you and the participants have encountered Jesus in Sacred Scripture and Sacred Tradition, in prayer experiences and learning group activities, the light of faith has grown within, and is reflected in words and actions.

In Today's Session ... During this last day of the Summer Program, the children will have the opportunity to spend time together in their learning groups, and to participate in a We Are Disciples event where they will meet members of the parish community and of the community at large who exemplify discipleship.

My Planning Notes
DAY 15

_____

_____

_____

_____

_____

_____

_____

_____

_____

AT A GLANCE DAY 15   **CHAPTERS 17 - 24**

Enriching the Lesson Activities	Chapter 17, page 263	Chapter 18, page 275	Chapter 19, page 287	Chapter 20, page 299	Chapter 21, page 315	Chapter 22, page 327	Chapter 23, page 339	Chapter 24, page 351
Grade 1	☐ Performing a Puppet Skit ☐ Sharing Words of Thanks and Praise ☐ Literature Connection	☐ Learning "Stop, Think, Decide" ☐ Keeping a Journal ☐ Literature Connection	☐ Making Collages about Respect ☐ Pantomiming People Showing Respect ☐ Literature Connection	☐ Charting Our Talents ☐ Literature Connection	☐ Taking Part in a Helping Hand ☐ Role-Playing a Scripture Story ☐ Literature Connection	☐ Making Coupon Books of Kindness ☐ Tracking Acts of Respect ☐ Literature Connection	☐ Acting Out an Echo Pantomime ☐ Being a Good Neighbor ☐ Literature Connection	☐ Solving an Our Father Puzzle ☐ Literature Connection
Grade 2	☐ Creating a Picture Story about Good Choices ☐ Pantomiming Acts of Kindness ☐ Literature Connection	☐ Art Activity: The Great Commandment ☐ Making Prayer Stories ☐ Literature Connection	☐ Making a "Happiness" Mobile ☐ Writing Letters of Thanks ☐ Literature Connection	☐ Collecting Food for Those in Need ☐ Discovering a World of Justice	☐ Holding a "Wise Choice" Party ☐ Making Care for Creation Posters ☐ Drawing Pictures of Peace	☐ Role-Play Doing the Right Thing ☐ Literature Connection	☐ Creating a Peace Blessing ☐ Writing Peacemaking Stories ☐ Literature Connection	☐ Preparing the Way for the Kingdom of God ☐ A Year of Faith Stories
Grade 3	☐ Reflecting on "Amazing Grace" ☐ Making Sympathy Cards ☐ Literature Connection	☐ Making Ten Commandment Puzzles ☐ Making Commandment Signposts ☐ Literature Connection	☐ A Respecting New Life Project ☐ Making Commandment Signposts ☐ Literature Connection	☐ Making Great Commandment Collages ☐ Literature Connection	☐ Performing Skits about Saint Paul ☐ Writing Letters to Missionary Orders ☐ Literature Connection	☐ Making Heart-Shaped Symbols ☐ Making Collages about Living Our Faith ☐ Literature Connection	☐ Pantomime the Beatitudes ☐ Discovering the Beatitudes in the News ☐ Literature Connection	☐ Making Prayer Spinners ☐ Literature Connection
Grade 4	☐ Storyboards about Free Will ☐ Acting Out Feelings ☐ Using a Word Web	☐ Rewriting Beatitudes ☐ Creating "True Happiness" Cards ☐ Conducting Interviews about Happiness	☐ Pantomiming the Cardinal Virtues ☐ Creating Diamante Poems ☐ Illustrating Lenten Posters	☐ Playing a Ten Commandments Game ☐ Comparing Headlines	☐ Designing Commandments Posters ☐ Keeping Sunday as a Family Day ☐ Word Web: Worshipping God	☐ Living the Fourth Commandment ☐ Creating "Respect" Door Hangers ☐ Designing Symbols	☐ Listening Game: The Problem with Gossip ☐ Designing a Web Site Home Page ☐ Frozen Snapshots about the Commandments	☐ Creating Symbols of God the Father ☐ Role-Playing a Favorite Scripture Story
Grade 5	☐ Creating Photographic Scenes ☐ Creating Symbols for Grace ☐ Role-Playing Cheerleaders for Holiness	☐ Creating Character Maps ☐ Grading Television ☐ Directing a Sitcom	☐ Jesus' Family Tree ☐ Creating Symbols for the Covenant ☐ Role-Playing a Scripture Story	☐ Making Beatitude Pennants ☐ Acting as Roving Reporters	☐ Rewriting the Commandments ☐ Creating a Commandment Poster ☐ Writing a Recipe to Keep Sunday Holy	☐ Writing Lyrics to a Song ☐ Creating Commandment Posters ☐ Creating Word Puzzles	☐ Creating a Motto ☐ Creating Commandment Posters ☐ Writing a Recipe	☐ Praying with Gestures ☐ Writing Welcome Letters
Grade 6	☐ Creating Portraits of Holiness ☐ A Job Description for Life ☐ Organizing a Food Drive	☐ Designing Proverb Bumper Stickers ☐ Solving Moral Dilemmas ☐ Creating Conscience Cartoons	☐ Mapping Qualities of a Disciple ☐ Making a Class Rules Banner ☐ Designing Friendship Prayer Cards	☐ Creating a Happiness Word Web ☐ Creating CDs about Holy People	☐ Creating Scrolls ☐ Re-enacting the Story of the Golden Calf ☐ Role-Playing Commandment Dilemmas	☐ Creating Heritage Booklets ☐ Creating a Discussion Web ☐ Using a Graphic Organizer	☐ Reviewing Faith Vocabulary ☐ Role-Playing Moral Dilemmas ☐ Affirming One Another	☐ Writing Prayers of Adoration ☐ Creating a Cinquain

Getting Started

In Advance

❏ Invite guests for today's "We Are Disciples" event. During this second part of the session, members of the parish and/or broader community will share with the children how they follow Jesus' command: Be My Disciples. One simple way to organize this event is to have the children rotate in groups from station to station, visiting and interacting with the guests to learn and ask questions about their discipleship.

❏ Schedule a time with your catechists to plan for this session. As on Days 5 and 10, the children will participate in hands-on, interactive learning activities focused around their chapter learning, Catholic Social Teaching, and Liturgical Year lessons. They will also participate in the "We Are Disciples" event during the second part of the session. You will want to include your catechists in the planning of these activities.

❏ If you have chosen the Friday afternoon/evening option for Days 5, 10, and 15 with a potluck community meal, be sure to send out reminders to the families and larger community with details about the time, the place, and the potluck meal.

❏ Determine the Activity Center format. You can plan age- or grade- level activities using the smaller meeting spaces for each group, or you can organize the large group meeting space as a Learning Center where the children rotate in small groups from one activity to the next.

❏ Determine the number of activities and leadership you will need for today's session.

• The number of activities you choose will depend on the number of participants in your program, and the leadership available to facilitate the activities. Consider asking youth from the parish to help set up and facilitate the day's activities.

• Organize the activities by grade level or by age-level groupings (primary, intermediate, or older children). Catechists from several grades can work together. You can plan a mix of age-specific and multi-age activities.

AT A GLANCE CATHOLIC SOCIAL TEACHING

Catholic Social Teaching Activities	Unit 5, page 299	Unit 6, page 351
Grade 1	❏ A Helping Project	❏ Making Prayer Calendars
Grade 2	❏ Respect for Our Elders	❏ Solidarity with Others
Grade 3	❏ Creating Slogans about Human Dignity	❏ Making Prayer Coupons
Grade 4	❏ Recipes for Human Dignity	❏ Researching Examples of Care for the Human Family
Grade 5	❏ Working for the Kingdom	❏ Writing Letters to Those Who Serve
Grade 6	❏ Living the Beatitudes	❏ Imitating Faith-Filled People

❏ Choose which learning activities will be a part of the interactive learning center. Refer to the grids on pages 123 and 124 for an overview of the many activities to choose from.

- Plan enough activities to fill a one-hour time frame. Choose activities best suited for your group. Some are suitable for all grade levels, some would work for age- level groups, and yet others would work nicely with older children helping the younger children. The Enriching the Lesson, Catholic Social Teaching, and Liturgical Year lessons work well as presented in the Catechist Guides, but the catechists can also use them as a starting point for their own creativity.

- The key is to aim for variety, creativity, and a bit of fun. Include a mix of language and music-related activities, person-related activities, and object-related activities. For more information and examples of each type, refer to 8 Kinds of Smart on page 27 in the Catechist Guide, and Activity Ideas on pages 18 and 19 in this manual. With your catechists, review and choose from the following:

Enriching the Lesson. Choose from the activities that appear at the end of Chapters 17 through 24 in the Catechist Guides, or create and plan similar types of activities. (See a listing of the Enriching the Lesson Activities on page 121.)

Catholic Social Teaching. Choose from activities that appear on page 299 (Unit 5: Life and Dignity of the Human Person), and page 351 (Unit 6: Solidarity of the Human Family) in the Catechist Guides. (See a listing on page 122).

The Liturgical Year. Consider including The Ascension of the Lord and Pentecost Sunday in the Learning Center, or other liturgical feasts and seasons not covered on Day 5 or Day 10.

❏ Decide how the children will process through the activities. Will you form small age- or grade- level groups that will travel together through the activities? Will you allow the children to choose from among the activities?

❏ Set up the large group meeting space. For the icebreaker Tic-Tac-Toe game, use masking tape to create a tic-tac-toe board at least 6 ft. by 6 ft. in size. Write X's on sheets of construction paper and O's on additional sheets..

❏ Set up the Interactive Gallery or showcase space where the children will display their work (arts and crafts, worksheets, etc.), and where they will present (if applicable) role-plays, puppet shows, stories, or skits.

❏ Prepare the prayer environment.

❏ Gather materials for all of the activities

❏ Collect one set of Faith Vocabulary/Faith Words cards from each age- or grade-level group for the eight chapters. You will use these in the Get Focused activity.

❏ Create a large Be My Disciples wall by posting the We Believe, We Worship and We Live walls in the large group meeting space where all can see them. By the end of the Summer Session, the children will have signed each of these three walls. Post the Disciple Power collage you have created during the three weeks.

❏ Collect children's activities and projects of the past three weeks to create a gallery which showcases and displays their work and learning.

❏ Optional: Assign someone to be the photographer or videographer for the Be My Disciples Digital Scrapbook (see pages 18-19). Set up the digital scrapbook to be showing as the children enter the session.

Materials

❏ Bible, candle, cross, cloth for prayer space

❏ Materials for activities in the Learning Center

❏ CD player and Be My Disciples Music CD

❏ Optional: projector, screen for Digital Scrapbook

WELCOME

You and the catechists should be on hand to greet the children when they arrive, especially on this last day of the program.

ICEBREAKER

• Invite all of the children to gather in the large meeting space.

• Play Tic Tac Toe (see Day 5 warm-up), this time using questions based on the content in Units 5 and 6.

LET'S GET FOCUSED

• Using the set of Faith Vocabulary/Faith Words cards you have collected from each of the age- or grade- level groups, play a Jeopardy-style game. Draw a card, and read aloud the definition of the word that appears on one side of it. Invite volunteers to give the response in the form of a question. For example: "The First Commandment calls on us to love and honor him." Response: "Who is God?." Be sure to call on both younger and older children.

• Call out some of the Disciple Power virtues that the children explored during the first four sessions (refer to the Disciple Power collage). Have them offer examples of concrete ways they have practiced the virtues.

• Tell the children that the theme of this session is Be My Disciples. Give them a moment to think about what it means to be disciples of Jesus. Ask: Where do I see disciples of Jesus at work in the world? Invite several volunteers to share with the large group. Transition into the opening prayer.

Ask the children to bow their heads, close their eyes for a brief moment, and remember that God is present with them in this time and place.

• Pray together the Sign of the Cross.

• Invite a child to read aloud John 8:31 from the Bible.

• Pose this question: What are the ways we can live as disciples of Jesus?

 Play "We are Disciples" (instrumental version) from the *Be My Disciples* Music CD while the children reflect on the question.

• Invite volunteers to share ways we can live as Jesus' disciples.

• End the prayer by praying together the Our Father.

DISCOVER, Part One

INTRODUCE

• Briefly review some of the major faith concepts that appear on the Be My Disciples wall. Tell the children that today they will have the opportunity to express what they have learned in art, crafts, storytelling, and other creative activities.

• Provide a brief orientation for the session. During this orientation you can describe the various learning activities and how the children will process through them. Tell them about (and introduce) the guests who will share with them today.

TEACH, REINFORCE, CONNECT

• Invite the children to join with their learning groups. Their catechists and leaders will be their guides as they travel through the learning stations set up in the Activity Center.

• Allow approximately one hour for the children to visit the activity stations.

• Have the children bring the art, crafts, worksheets, etc. that they worked on during the first part of the session to their grades' section of the Interactive Gallery before moving into the break.

LET'S TAKE A BREAK!

When the age- or grade-level groups have completed their work with the first part of the day, invite them to join together with all of the children in the program for refreshments and play time. (Note: Some groups may finish before others. To avoid distractions for the groups still meeting, if possible, set up the break time activities away from the meeting spaces.)

DISCOVER, Part Two

INTRODUCE

Invite all of the children back into the large group meeting space. Have the children quietly file past the Be My Disciples Wall. Then, ask them which items on the wall they have focused on in their activities thus far today.

- Invite them to sign the We Live section of the wall.

- Tell the children that they are now going to meet guests from the community who will share with them how they live as disciples.

WE ARE DISCIPLES!

Facilitate the "We Are Disciples" experience. Give the children plenty of time to meet the guests, to find out about their work and ministries in the parish and community, and to ask questions.

LET'S WRAP IT UP!

REINFORCE

- Invite all of the children to gather, with their catechists, in the main meeting space.

- Quickly go around the room and ask volunteers to fill in the blanks (out loud) for sentences such as: My favorite moment during this Summer Program was _____. The most important thing I learned was _____. My favorite Bible story is _____. I want to practice the Disciple Power virtue of _____.

- Direct everyone's attention once again to the Be My Disciples wall. Ask the learning groups to come up with a Top Ten list of things they learned during the past three weeks about what it means to be a disciple of Jesus.

WE REMEMBER

- Invite each group to present its Top Ten list.

- Ask the children to spend several minutes in remembering some of the Faith Choices they have made over the past weeks. You may want to guide their reflection by naming some of the Faith Choices that are in the various grade levels and chapters.

- Invite the children to make one more Faith Choice to conclude the program: "I choose to be a disciple of Jesus. I will be a disciple of Jesus by _____."

WE PRAY

 Begin and end today's prayer with the theme song, "We are Disciples" from the *Be My Disciples* Music Program. It appears on each grade level CD.

- Have the participants gather in the prayer space.

We Pray

- Light a candle and pray together the Sign of the Cross.

Leader: God our Creator, we are thankful for the time we have shared these past weeks. Be with us as we pray together. Amen.

Reader: (Read Luke 11:1-4.)

Leader: May we remember now, in the quiet of our hearts, the Faith Choices we have each made to be Jesus' disciples.

(Pause for a moment of quiet.)

(Have the children echo the following after you.)

Leader: Guide us, Lord, and be with us always. We are your disciples.

All: Guide us, Lord . . . ..

- Join hands and pray the Lord's Prayer aloud together. Conclude by sharing a Sign of Peace with each other.

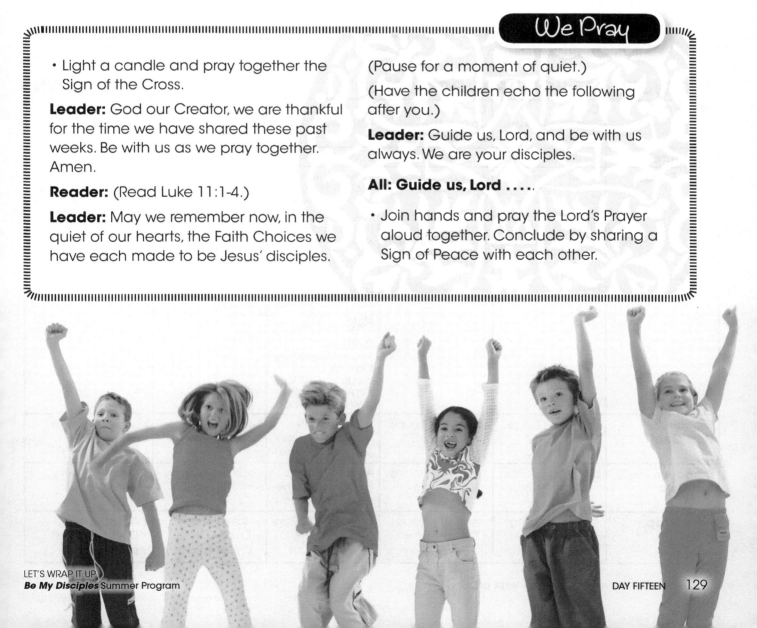

Be My Disciples *Alternative Model*

The Two-Week + At Home Option

The two-week option provides age-appropriate catechesis for children in peer groups at the parish, and parent facilitation of catechesis using the *Be My Disciples* At Home Family Guide.

Catechesis at the parish covers the first two chapters of each Unit in each of the three themes (We Believe, We Worship, We Live). Families explore the two remaining chapters in each Unit using the At Home Family Guide.

Note that if you choose this program model, the children will not complete the *Be My Disciples* curriculum in the sessions at the parish. This model requires parents and families to facilitate half of the curriculum at home with their children using the *Be My Disciples* At Home Family Guide.

At the Parish

With minor adjustments, the sessions you hold at the parish in the two-week model correlate to sessions in the three-week model. Follow the session plans presented in the three-week Summer Program that correlate as follows. We've noted where you will need to make adaptations in the day's session outline.

TWO WEEK + AT HOME PROGRAM MODEL   WEEK ONE

Week One	Day 1 Teach Me Your Ways	Day 2 Jesus, the Messiah	Day 3 I Believe!	Day 4 Give Thanks	Day 5 Increase Our Faith
Scripture	Psalm 86:11	Matthew 16:16	John 20:26–31	Psalm 118:29	Luke 17:5-6
Faith Focus	•God reveals himself to us; God shows us the way to himself. •God gives us the gift of faith to help us know and believe in him.	•Jesus is the Son of God, the Messiah. •The Paschal Mystery is the mystery of Jesus' Passion, Death, Resurrection and Ascension.	•The Church professes belief in the Holy Trinity. •We celebrate the liturgical seasons of Advent, Christmas, and Ordinary Time. **Liturgical Year:** Advent, Christmas, Epiphany, Ordinary Time **Catholic Social Teaching:** Care for God's creation; Call to family, community, and participation	•In the celebration of Confirmation, we use specific words and actions. •The Fruits of the Spirit show that we live in and follow the Spirit.	•Our participation in the sacramental life of the Church increases our faith •Our families are families of faith.
Discover, Part One	Learning Groups • Chapter 1	Learning Groups • Chapter 5	Activity Centers (see Day 5 in the 3-week program)	Learning Groups • Chapter 9	Learning Groups • Chapter 13
Discover, Part Two	Learning Groups • Chapter 2	Learning Groups • Chapter 6	Activity Centers (see Day 5 in the 3-week program)	Learning Groups • Chapter 10	Learning Groups • Chapter 14
Let's Wrap It Up	• Activity sharing • Disciple Power presentations	• Activity sharing • Disciple Power presentations	Interactive Gallery • Displays • Presentations	• Activity sharing • Disciple Power presentations	• Activity sharing • Disciple Power presentations

TWO WEEK + AT HOME PROGRAM MODEL

Week Two	Day 6 Light of the World	Day 7 Put On Love	Day 8 Love Never Fails	Day 9 Be My Disciples!	Day 10 Give Glory to God
Scripture	Matthew 5:14, 16	Colossians 3:14	1 Corinthians 13: 4-5, 7-8a	John 8:31	1 Corinthians 10:31
Faith Focus	•We are called to be the light of the world. •The Sacraments nourish us to be lights in the world.	•We are called to holiness and to "put on love."	•As Jesus' disciples we are called to lives of love.	•We respond to Jesus' invitation: Be My Disciples! **Liturgical Year:** Ascension, Pentecost **Catholic Social Teaching:** Life and dignity of the human person; Solidarity of the human family.	•The Sacraments give us the grace we need to do everything for the glory of God. •We celebrate and share in the Eucharist. **Liturgical Year:** Triduum/Holy Thursday **Catholic Social Teaching:** Dignity of work and the rights of workers; Option for the poor and vulnerable
Discover, Part One	Activity Centers •Enriching the Lesson •Catholic Social Teaching •Liturgical Year	Learning Groups • Chapter 17	Learning Groups • Chapter 21	Activity Centers •Enriching the Lesson •Catholic Social Teaching •Liturgical Year	Activity Centers •Catholic Social Teaching •Liturgical Year
Discover, Part Two	Activity Centers •Enriching the Lesson •Catholic Social Teaching •Liturgical Year	Learning Groups • Chapter 18	Learning Groups • Chapter 22	Activity Centers •Enriching the Lesson	Learning Groups •We Celebrate the Mass *(Families and Parish Community invited)* •Mass Preparation •Mass
Let's Wrap It Up	Activity Centers Interactive Gallery •Displays •Presentations	• Activity sharing • Disciple Power presentations	• Activity sharing • Disciple Power presentations	Interactive Gallery •Displays •Presentations	•Potluck Meal *(Families and Parish Community invited)*

Two-Week Program Sessions Correlation	Three-Week Program Sessions
DAY 1 correlates to	DAY 1 session (see pages 28-35)
DAY 2 correlates to	DAY 3 session (see pages 42-47)
DAY 3 correlates to	DAY 5 session (see pages 54-61)
DAY 4 correlates to	DAY 6 session (see pages 64-69)
DAY 5 correlates to	DAY 8 session (see pages 76-81)
DAY 6 correlates to	Adapt DAY 9 and DAY 10 sessions (see pages 82-95) For Welcome activities and opening prayer, use Day 9. For Discover Part 1, use Day 10. For Discover Part 2, repeat Day 10, Part 1 (replace Mass Preparation and Mass with Activity Centers organized around Enriching the Lesson, Catholic Social Teaching, and Liturgical Year).
DAY 7 correlates to	Use Day 11 session (see pages 98-103)
DAY 8 correlates to	Use Day 13 session (see pages 110-115)
DAY 9 correlates to	Adapt Day 15 session (see pages 122-129)
DAY 10 correlates to	Adapt Day 10 session (see pages 88-95). For Discover Part 1, use remaining Catholic Social Teaching and Liturgical Year. Include a Potluck Meal at the end of the session if desired.

Be My Disciples Alternative Model

At Home

The two-week program model places responsibility for half of the *Be My Disciples* curriculum in the hands of parents. Each family will need a copy of the *Be My Disciples* At Home Family Guide, as well as the student books for the children. Parents will work with their children on the chapters not covered in the two-week program. The At Home approach gives parents the flexibility to work through the chapters with their children at their own pace.

At Home Family Guide	Unit and Chapters	Unit and Chapters
We Believe	Unit 1, Chapters 3 and 4	Unit 2, Chapters 7 and 8
We Worship	Unit 3, Chapters 11 and 12	Unit 4, Chapters 15 and 16
We Live	Unit 5, Chapters 19 and 20	Unit 6, Chapters 23 and 24

We encourage you to establish some measure of mutual accountability and communication between the parish and the parents. One approach is to enter into a covenant or a contract which outlines the partnership, and the responsibilities of each party. You can view a sample contract for the Summer Program at *BeMyDisciples*.com in the section for Program Directors.

Multiple resources are available for you to support parents and maximize at-home learning. See pages 24-25 and page 131 for more information.

AT A GLANCE Resources for Parents and Families

Assessment Tools
Use these reproducible masters to create an assessment portfolio with chapter and unit tests and other assessment instructions.

Additional Activities
Parents can enhance the lessons with these reproducible activities that extend their children's learning.

BeMyDisciples.com
A wealth of resources that connect with the student books and enhance the learning experience at home. Includes interactive chapter reviews, children's activities and games, a weekly continuing story, a tour of a Catholic Church, Gospel reflections, and other resources for parents and families.

Intergenerational and Parent Workshops
We also strongly recommend that you invite parents and families to several intergenerational and parent workshops throughout the year (see page 131).

Be My Disciples Additional Suggestions

Partnering with Parents and Families

The Christian family offers the first and best environment for growth in faith, and the first experience of Christian community. The Catholic Church views the role of parents and families in the religious formation of children as both a privilege and an obligation. In the Rite of Baptism, Catholic parents are clearly reminded that they have the responsibility "of training [children] in the practice of the faith" (*Rite of Baptism for Children* 39).

The *Be My Disciples* Summer Program engages and supports parents and families through the With My Family take-home page that is part of every student chapter, through a variety of projects and activities within the text and online at *BeMyDisciples*.com, and through the program being offered at the parish itself.

Intergenerational Workshops

Throughout the year, whether you schedule the three-week or two-week program, plan several gatherings that bring together parents and families. If you offer a school-year religious education program at your parish, be sure to invite the families of those who participate in the Summer Program to any workshops or gatherings you hold for them.

Liturgical Year Workshops

The *Be My Disciples* curriculum includes fifteen Liturgical Year lessons that, when grouped together by season, could become the basis for intergenerational gatherings using the Activity Center approach. Here's one example of how you could group Liturgical Year lessons into seasonal workshops for families.

Seasonal Workshop for Families	Liturgical Year Sessions from *Be My Disciples*
Advent/Christmas	Advent, Christmas, Epiphany
Lent	Ash Wednesday, Lent
Holy Week/Triduum/Easter Sunday	Palm Sunday, Triduum/Holy Thursday, Triduum/ Good Friday, Triduum/Easter
Easter Season/Pentecost	The Ascension of the Lord, Pentecost Sunday
Ordinary Time	The Liturgical Year, All Saints
Marian Feast Days	The Immaculate Conception, Our Lady of Guadalupe, Mary, the Holy Mother of God

Intergenerational Gathering: Households of Faith

This session, which is included in the *Be My Disciples* Parish Director's Manual, page 89, is an intergenerational gathering that could take place near the opening of the *Be My Disciples* Summer Program. It is an opportunity for parents and other caregivers to gather with the children and reflect on the meaning of being a household of faith.

Disciple Power

WEEK ONE

Grade Level	DAY 1 Disciple Power	DAY 2 Disciple Power	DAY 3 Disciple Power	DAY 4 Disciple Power
Grade 1	Faithful Generosity	Wonder Kindness	Courage Hope	Counsel Reverence
Grade 2	Respect Hospitality	Wonder Honor	Mercy Sacrifice	Generosity Goodness
Grade 3	Love Generosity	Honor Justice	Hope Joy	Faithfulness Humility
Grade 4	Truthfulness Faith	Trust Hope	Love Courage	Wisdom Understanding
Grade 5	Knowledge Reverence	Wonder & Awe Joy	Faithfulness Hope	Courage Peace
Grade 6	Perseverance in faith Knowledge	Wonder & Awe Justice	Humility Mercy	Counsel Peace

WEEK TWO

Grade Level	DAY 6 Disciple Power	DAY 7 Disciple Power	DAY 8 Disciple Power	DAY 9 Disciple Power
Grade 1	Prudence Hospitality	Goodness Fidelity	Patience Peace	Perseverance Wisdom
Grade 2	Piety Faith	Knowledge Forgiveness	Love Compassion	Thankfulness Courage
Grade 3	Patience Love	Fortitude Kindness	Understanding Goodness	Chastity Wisdom
Grade 4	Wonder & Awe Truthfulness	Knowledge Joy	Kindness Forgiveness	Compassion Holiness
Grade 5	Perseverance Generosity	Understanding Charity	Mercy Kindness	Faith Humility
Grade 6	Diligence Modesty	Fortitude Faithfulness	Self-control Gentleness	Patience Chastity

WEEK THREE

Grade Level	DAY 11 Disciple Power	DAY 12 Disciple Power	DAY 13 Disciple Power	DAY 14 Disciple Power
Grade 1	Understanding Knowledge	Temperance Justice	Joy Gentleness	Charity Humility
Grade 2	Kindness Fortitude	Obedience Justice	Humility Joy	Trust Hope
Grade 3	Piety Gentleness	Self-control Prudence	Reverence Knowledge	Perseverance Obedience
Grade 4	Prudence Generosity	Justice Fortitude	Diligence Respect	Mercy Charity
Grade 5	Goodness Prudence	Obedience Justice	Meekness Temperance	Integrity Piety
Grade 6	Understanding Prudence	Charity Joy	Piety Temperance	Generosity Hope

CREDITS

p8 © Mary Wessel; p8 ©Thinkstock; p8 ©Robert Churchill/Getty; p13 ©Monkey Business Images/Shutterstock; p17 ©Diego Cervo/Shutterstock; p20 © Getty Images/Thinkstock; p20 © Jupiterimages/Thinkstock; p21 © Digital Vision/Thinkstock; p25 © Mary Wessel; p28 © Stockbyte/Thinkstock; p29 © Getty Images/Thinkstock; p30 © Mary Wessel; p32 © Thinkstock; p33 © Brand X Pictures/Thinkstock; p35 © R. Gino Santa Maria/Shutterstock; p36 © Brand X Pictures/Thinkstock; p37 © wavebreakmedia/Shutterstock; p38 ©Monkey Business Images/Shutterstock; p40 ©Tom Wang/Shutterstock; p42 ©Monkey Business Images/Shutterstock; p43 ©Yuri Arcurs/Shutterstock; p44 ©Patrick Foto/Shutterstock; p44 ©Shutterstock; p46 ©Rob Marmion/Shutterstock; p46 ©MANDY GODBEHEAR/Shutterstock; p49 ©Stockbyte/Thinkstock; p49 ©Monkey Business Images/Shutterstock; p50 ©Mary Wessel; p52 ©Naypong/Shutterstock; p55 ©ampyang/Shutterstock; p58 ©Monkey Business Images/Shutterstock; p59 ©Monkey Business Images/Shutterstock; p60 ©Brand X Pictures/Thinkstock; p61 ©Comstock/Thinkstock; p64 ©Pressmaster/Shutterstock; p68 © Getty Images/Thinkstock; p65 ©Monkey Business Images/Shutterstock; p70 ©Monkey Business Images/Shutterstock; p71 ©BlueOrange Studio/Shutterstock; p72 © Monkey Business Images/Shutterstock; p73 © Monkey Business Images/Shutterstock; p73 ©Rob Marmion/Shutterstock; p76 Andresr/Shutterstock; p77 © Mary Wessel; p78 © Monkey Business Images/Shutterstock; p80 © Thinkstock; p82 © Darrin Henry/Shutterstock; p83 ©Golden Pixels LLC/Shutterstock; p85 ©George Doyle/Thinkstock; p88 ©Pressmaster/Shutterstock; p91 ©Thinkstock; p92 ©Matka_Wariatka/Shutterstock; p93 ©Thinkstock; p94 ©Thinkstock; p95 ©Monkey Business Images/Shutterstock; p95 ©Jacek Chabraszewski/Shutterstock; p 98 ©Thinkstock; p100 ©Monkey Business Images/Shutterstock; p102 ©Beth Swanson/Shutterstock; p104 © Zurijeta/Shutterstock; p105 © Thinkstock; p106 © 2013 Masterfile Corporation; p108 ©forestpath/Shutterstock; p108 © Thinkstock; p110 © StockbrokerXtra/Alamy; p111 © Thinkstock; p112 © Andresr/Shutterstock; p112 © istockphoto; p116 © Monkey Business Images/Shutterstock; p116 ©Thinkstock; p117 © Mary Wessel; p118 © Andresr/Shutterstock; p118 © istockphoto; p120 ©Naypong/Shutterstock; p122 ©Thinkstock; p122 ©istockphoto; p126 © Lori Sparkia/Shutterstock; p 127 ©Thinkstock; p128 ©istockphoto; p129 ©BananaStock/Thinkstock; p134 ©Thinkstock; p135 © Agnieszka Kirinicjanow/Thinkstock